TEXTS AND STUDIES

CONTRIBUTIONS TO
BIBLICAL AND PATRISTIC LITERATURE

EDITED BY

J. ARMITAGE ROBINSON D.D.

HON. PH.D. GÖTTINGEN HON. D.D. HALLE
CANON OF WESTMINSTER

VOL. VII.

No. 2. S. EPHRAIM'S QUOTATIONS FROM
THE GOSPEL

S. EPHRAIM'S QUOTATIONS
FROM THE GOSPEL

COLLECTED AND ARRANGED

BY

F. CRAWFORD BURKITT M.A.

Wipf & Stock
PUBLISHERS
Eugene, Oregon

Wipf and Stock Publishers
199 W 8th Ave, Suite 3
Eugene, OR 97401

S. Ephraim's Quotations from the Gospel
By Burkitt, F.C.
ISBN: 1-59244-899-2
Publication date 9/29/2004
Previously published by Cambridge, 1901

PREFACE.

THIS book is an attempt to determine what text of the Gospels was used in the genuine works of S. Ephraim, and to investigate the bearing of his quotations upon the date of the Peshitta. S. Ephraim, commonly known as Ephraem Syrus, is the only one of the worthies of the Syriac-speaking Church whose name is well known both in the East and the West, and his surviving works, even when all doubtful and spurious pieces have been set on one side, are by themselves as voluminous as all the other remains of Syriac literature earlier than 400 AD. He himself died about 373 AD, so that any version of the Bible used by him must be at least as old as the fourth century.

In the first quarter of the fifth century the Gospel was extant in Syriac in three forms:

1. The *Syriac Vulgate*, now commonly called the *Peshitta*. This version is extant in numerous MSS, some even as old as the middle of the fifth century, and has been frequently printed. The text even of the most ancient MSS of this version differs but little from the printed editions, and such variations as exist are mostly concerned with spelling and questions of grammatical form. This is the version in ecclesiastical use among all the sects of Syriac-speaking Christians.

2. The *Evangelion da-Mepharreshe* (i.e. 'The Separated Gospels'), also called by the followers of the late Dr Hort the *Old Syriac*. Two MSS of this version are at present known to scholars,

viz. the Curetonian MS, discovered by Dr Cureton among the Nitrian MSS in the British Museum, and published by him in 1858; and the Sinai Palimpsest, discovered in 1892 by Mrs Lewis and Mrs Gibson of Cambridge at the Convent of S. Catharine on Mount Sinai, and published at Cambridge in 1894. In the following pages I have called Cureton's MS C, and the Sinai Palimpsest S. Both MSS are very ancient: I am inclined to ascribe S to the end of the 4th century, and C to the beginning of the 5th. In text, S and C differ widely from each other and from the Peshitta.

3. A third form of the Gospel in use among Syriac-speaking Christians during the 3rd and 4th centuries was the *Diatessaron*, a Harmony of the Four Gospels made by Tatian the disciple of Justin Martyr. The language in which this Harmony was originally drawn up is disputed and its early history obscure. No MS of it in any of its primitive forms is known to survive. Large fragments, however, are quoted in a Commentary on the Diatessaron, composed by S. Ephraim but extant only in an Armenian translation; and it is highly probable that most of the quotations in the works of Aphraates and some other early Syriac writers were taken from the Diatessaron, rather than from the Four Gospels. Besides these quotations there is also extant a complete text of the Diatessaron in Arabic, translated from a later form of the Syriac text in which the wording had been almost entirely assimilated to the Peshitta. The Arabic therefore enables us to reconstruct with some confidence the arrangement of the Diatessaron, but it gives us little information about the actual wording of it in early times. The wording of the Diatessaron, as it appears in S. Ephraim's Commentary, is very like that found in the MSS of the *Evangelion da-Mepharreshe*, though it is by no means identical with it.

In the West an echo of the Diatessaron may be said to survive in the *Codex Fuldensis*, a MS prepared by Victor, bishop of Capua about 540 AD. But the text is completely assimilated to the Latin Vulgate; and the order of the events, while agreeing in the main with the Arabic Harmony and the Commentary of S. Ephraim, has in many places been altered.

The relation of the Peshitta to the *Evangelion da-Mepharreshe* and of both to the Diatessaron has been a subject of controversy ever since the publication of the Curetonian text. According to Dr Hort the analogy between the Syriac and the Latin versions is complete. There was an 'Old Latin' Version or Versions current in the West, the MSS of which differed widely one from the other. Late in the 4th century, S. Jerome was commissioned by Pope Damasus to put an end to the confusion by preparing a Revised Version corrected from the Greek. The Gospels were published in 383 AD, and after a struggle this Revised Version superseded its predecessors. Dr Hort contended that the same thing must have happened in the East, and that the Curetonian (the only MS of the *Evangelion da-Mepharreshe* published during his lifetime) bore the same relation to the Peshitta that Codex Vercellensis (*a*) or Codex Veronensis (*b*) bears to the Latin Vulgate. No one supposes that S. Jerome used either of the particular MSS which we call *a* and *b* as the basis of his revision; but *a* and *b* were MSS of the same class as those which S. Jerome revised by means of his Greek MSS. Similarly the Curetonian MS, according to Dr Hort, was one of the same class as that which underlies the Peshitta text of the Gospels.

It was certainly a great confirmation of Dr Hort's view when, on the publication of the Sinai Palimpsest, this MS was found to be of the same kind as the Curetonian, while presenting a text very far from identical with it. Sometimes the Sinai Palimpsest agrees with the Peshitta against the Curetonian, more often it differs from both: in fact, it presents exactly the same phenomena as are exhibited in a greater or less degree by the mutual variations of the Latin Vulgate and any two codices of the Old Latin. But a successful prediction does not altogether prove a theory, and Dr Hort's theory of the Syriac Versions is open to the objection that it has the air of a deduction made not from the Syriac evidence but from a general theory of the history of the Greek text of the New Testament. At any rate it is not convincing to use the general theory to prove that the Curetonian is the Old Syriac (syr.vt), and then to appeal to the character of the Old Syriac text in support of the general theory. I am far from saying that this really was Dr Hort's procedure, but it was quite open for the critic who did not believe in the general theory to declare that Dr Hort "was obliged to account for the relation of the two [the Syriac Vulgate and the Curetonian] by the baseless supposition of an imaginary recension at Edessa" (Miller's *Scrivener*, vol. ii, p. 17).

We need not linger over the various counter-theories which have been advanced to explain the Curetonian text on the hypothesis that the Peshitta, practically in its present form, is very much older than the Fourth Century. Indeed it is of the essence of the plea raised by the defenders of the antiquity of the Peshitta N.T. that they have no need of a theory. "The Peshitto has the advantage of *possession*, and that too of fourteen centuries standing," said Dr Scrivener; and by this is meant the alleged use of the Peshitta N.T. by the Fathers of the Syriac-speaking Church back to and including S. Ephraim. The use of the Peshitta by Isaac of Antioch and the biographer of Rabbula, both writing in the middle of the 5th century, is undisputed. The real question is whether it can be traced beyond Rabbula.

The principal aim, therefore, of this book is to examine whether S. Ephraim's quotations of the Gospels were taken, as is commonly believed, from the Peshitta text. I have occasion so often to traverse the views of Mr G. H. Gwilliam, to whose critical edition of the Peshitta Gospels we are all looking forward, that it gives me great pleasure to be able to conclude this Preface by quoting words of his with which I can fully agree. Mr Gwilliam, after stating his belief that the complete Testament in use among the early Syrian Fathers must have been substantially the same as that known for centuries as the Peshitta, said in *Studia Biblica* i 168 f.: "This point can only be satisfactorily settled by an exhaustive examination of the quotations in the early Syriac writers. It is usually assumed that the quotations in St. Ephraem are made from the Peshito, but the question deserves full investigation, which should extend to all the early Syriac literature. It might be found that these writers employed, as their vernacular New Testament, some other version which has now perished, being succeeded by the Peshito, in the early years of the fifth century, but that has yet to be proved."

Caesarem appellasti? ad Caesarem ibis.

F. C. BURKITT.

ELTERHOLM, CAMBRIDGE.
September, 1901.

CONTENTS.

	PAGE
S. EPHRAIM'S QUOTATIONS FROM THE GOSPEL	1-58
Chief Editions of S. Ephraim's Works	3
The Sources of the Roman Edition	4
The Homilies in Cod. Vat. Syr. cxvii	20
List of the Genuine Writings of S. Ephraim	24, 25
List of Quotations from the Gospel	26, 27
Examination of S. Ephraim's Quotations	
from S. Matthew	28
from S. Mark .	37
from S. Luke	40
from S. John	48
S. Ephraim and the *Diatessaron*	56
Rabbula's revision of the Syriac N.T.	57
APPENDIX I: S. Ephraim's Quotations from the Prologue to the Fourth Gospel	59-65
APPENDIX II: On some of the less well attested works of S. Ephraim	66-74
APPENDIX III: On some writings wrongly ascribed to S. Ephraim	75-89
INDEX of Gospel Passages	90, 91

ERRATUM: p. 39, l. 15, *for* ܟܐܢܘܬܐ *read* ܡܟܐܢܘܬܐ

"*Anything which throws new light on the history of the text will be found in the end to throw new light on the history of Christianity.*"

SANDAY AND HEADLAM, *Commentary on the Epistle to the Romans*, p. lxxi.

S. EPHRAIM'S QUOTATIONS
FROM THE GOSPEL.

THE discussion of S. Ephraim's quotations from the Gospel cannot be other than a technical matter. It involves some rather complicated questions of Syriac bibliography and literary history, besides requiring a knowledge of the problems connected with the text of the *Diatessaron*. But the subject is of very great interest to all students of the history of the Bible in the Church, because the date we assign to the Peshitta New Testament largely depends upon the view we take of S. Ephraim's relation to this version.

I need hardly enlarge upon the importance of this date. The Peshitta N.T. is the sheet-anchor of the defenders of the Greek *Textus Receptus*: it is the great obstacle in the way both to the disciples of Westcott and Hort and to those who champion what are called 'Western' texts. The date and origin of the Peshitta is, or should be, also a subject of concern for students of Church History. Like the Latin Vulgate, and indeed to a far greater extent than the Latin Vulgate, it has a fixed text. It is a monument of ecclesiastical authority and ecclesiastical veneration, and its unchanged preservation testifies to persistent and unbroken reverence for the letter of the New Testament, continued even through schism and disruption. It is highly interesting therefore to determine how old this monument is, to ascertain from what date this care and veneration has been given by the Syriac-speaking Churches to the ecclesiastical text, and to inquire whether it was so treated on account of its apostolical antiquity.

It is well known that there are two schools of opinion about the date of the Peshitta N.T. The traditional opinion, now represented in England by Mr G. H. Gwilliam, places it in the second century: Dr Hort, on the other hand, put it between 250 and 350 AD (*Introd.* § 189 f.). Thus according to either view the Peshitta N.T. was extant in S. Ephraim's day, as he died about 373 AD. The main object of this present Essay is to point to a very different conclusion. I do not think there is any real trace of the use of the Peshitta Gospel text in the genuine works of S. Ephraim; on the contrary, I believe that the version of the N.T. which we know by the name of "the Pĕshiṭtâ," and which is preserved in so many ancient MSS from the fifth century downwards, is the result of a revision made and promulgated by Rabbula, bishop of Edessa from 411—435 AD.[1]

The most useful investigation of S. Ephraim's quotations hitherto published is that of Mr F. H. Woods in the third volume of *Studia Biblica*, pp. 105—138. Mr Woods finds very decided traces of the Peshitta in S. Ephraim's writings. He says: "Even a cursory glance at the Table [i.e. pp. 120—138] makes it quite evident that Ephrem in the main used the Peshitto text" (p. 107). And again: "as a fact we find very few variants from the Peshitto according with what appears to be the text of the Diatessaron" (p. 115). This view is so inconsistent with the results at which I have arrived that there must be somewhere a fundamental difference between his method and that pursued here. The difference can be stated in a few words. As Mr Woods himself tells us, he trusted to the printed text of the Roman Edition, both for the text of S. Ephraim and the genuineness of the writings ascribed to him: if I have come to opposite conclusions, it is because of the evidence afforded by the MS authority upon which the Roman Edition is based.

[1] See *Journal of Theological Studies* i 571. To save misconception, it is well to state at once that the *Old Testament* Peshitta is universally acknowledged to be of great antiquity. It is in any case older than Aphraates and S. Ephraim, as may be seen from their quotations *passim*.

The chief editions of S. Ephraim's works are :—

1. THE ROMAN EDITION. *Sancti Patris nostri Ephraem Syri Opera Omnia...in sex tomos distributa*, etc. The three volumes of the Greek version of Ephraim appeared between 1732 and 1746, while the three Syriac volumes appeared between 1737 and 1743. These three Syriac volumes (quoted in agreement with Mr Woods's notation as iv, v, and vi) were edited by the Maronite Peter Mobárak (Petrus Benedictus), S. J., and after his death by S..E. Assemani.

The Roman Edition gives no information about the MSS used, except that they were those of the Vatican and other Roman Libraries. To supply this defect we must go to the *Bibliotheca Orientalis* of J. S. Assemani and the magnificent Catalogue of the Syriac MSS in the Vatican published by J. S. and S. E. Assemani.[1]

2. OVERBECK. *S. Ephraemi Syri, Rabulae Episcopi Edesseni, Balaei Aliorumque Opera Selecta...primus edidit J. Josephus Overbeck*, Oxford, 1865. The work contains a number of hitherto unedited pieces of various ages, without translation.[2]

3. CARMINA NISIBENA...*primus edidit Dr Gustavus Bickell*, Leipzig, 1866. "These poems, which deal in great part with the history of Nisibis and its bishops and of adjacent cities...were composed, according to Bickell, between the years 350 and 370 or thereabouts" (Wright's *Syriac Literature*, p. 36).

4. LAMY. *Sancti Ephraem Syri Hymni et Sermones ..edidit... Thomas Josephus Lamy*, 3 vols., Louvain, 1882—9. These volumes give us a good deal that is certainly not of the fourth century, but they also contain the *Sermo de Domino nostro* (Lamy i 145—274, ii pp. xxi—xxiii), which is for textual and doctrinal purposes perhaps the most important work of S. Ephraim which survives.

---

[1] It was not the least of Mr Bradshaw's services to the Cambridge University Library that he secured for it a copy of this exceedingly rare and costly work.

[2] I have heard that the proofs were corrected by Dr William Wright, who was then preparing his great Catalogue of the British Museum MSS. This at least would account for the accuracy of the printed text.

4   S. EPHRAIM'S QUOTATIONS.

To these we must add the Commentary on the *Diatessaron*, now extant in an Armenian version. It is convenient to cite this work by the pages of Moesinger's Latin translation (Venice, 1876), though the Biblical quotations have been more accurately rendered from the Armenian into English by Canon Armitage Robinson (best given in pp. 75—119 of Dr Hamlyn Hill's *Dissertation on the Gospel Commentary of S. Ephraem the Syrian*, Edinburgh, 1896).

The Sources of the Roman Edition.

The Roman Edition of S. Ephraim is one of the most confusing and misleading works ever published. The Latin translation is an inaccurate and verbose paraphrase, there is no index of any kind except the scanty table of contents at the beginning of each volume, and the only indication of MS sources is a short Epistle to the reader. The actual editing of the Syriac is equally bad. The readings of the MSS are sometimes arbitrarily changed without any warning, while the principles upon which the various hymns and homilies have been selected and arranged are impossible to discover. Side by side with a homily of undoubted genuineness taken from a 6th century MS we find another which only bears S. Ephraim's name through a slip of the pen of a 12th century scribe, and this ill-matched pair is placed next hymns, whose claim to inclusion is that they form part of the book of daily offices now used by the Maronites. To draw any critical conclusions from hymns of this last class is comparable with attempting to employ the "Prayer of St. Chrysostom" as an authority for the text in use at Antioch in the 4th century.[1]

---

[1] In the *Journal of Theological Studies* i 569 ff. I pointed out one instance where a close agreement of S. Ephraim with the Curetonian has been transformed in the Roman Edition into an agreement with the Peshitta. Another is to be found in vi 16 F, where the Edition has ܬܐܘܡܐ ܘܠܗ (i.e. 'and him, Thomas'). The true text, given *from the same* MS in Assemani's *Bibl. Orient.* I 101, is ܬܐܘܡܐ ܠܝܗܘܕܐ (i.e. 'and Judas Thomas'). This also is the reading of B.M. Add. 12176 (*fol.* 5vb), a MS of the 5th or 6th century. The double name *Judas Thomas* is specially characteristic of Old Syriac documents, and is found in Joh xiv 22 *C*.

INDEX TO THE ROMAN EDITION. 5

The only way to make critical use of the Roman Edition is to give what ought from the first to have formed part of it, *viz.* an Index shewing the sources from which the single pieces are taken. This I shall now do, adding at the same time the numbers and dates of MSS in the British Museum in which certain of the pieces are preserved. It should be remembered that the best MSS in the Vatican came from the same source as most of those in the British Museum, i.e the great Syriac Library of S. Mary Deipara in the Nitrian Desert.

Index to the Roman Edition.

In the following Index the left-hand column gives the general titles of the groups of writings: where a line of Syriac is given, it is the first line of the several Homilies or Hymns of the miscellaneous collections according to the order in which they occur in the Roman Edition. The second column gives the page and volume of the three Syro-Latin volumes of the Roman Edition. The third column gives the reference to J. S. Assemani's *Bibliotheca Orientalis*: in this the big Roman numeral refers to the sections under which the account of S. Ephraim's works is there grouped. The fourth column gives the number and section of the Vatican MS from which the work was edited, followed by its date in round brackets, according to the Assemanis' *Catalogue*: thus "cxvii 153 (xii°)" means the 153rd section of Cod. Vat. Syr. cxvii, as numbered in the Roman Catalogue, the MS being there ascribed to the 12th century. The last column gives the number of the Additional MS or MSS in the British Museum in which the piece is also found, together with its date and the page where it is described in Wright's *Catalogue*. If the piece be ascribed to any particular author, his name is given in square brackets; if no name be given, it is ascribed to S. Ephraim in the MS.

Title, or First Line.	Edit. Rom.
Commentary on Genesis	IV 1
Notes on Genesis[1]	IV 116
Commentary on Exodus	IV 194
Notes on the rest of the O.T.[1]	IV 236 —V 315

Sermones Exegetici (V 316—395)

ܚܠܒ ܕܡܢ ܠܒܬܐ.	V 316
ܐܕܡ ܐܝܟ ܘܐܬܒܣܡ.	V 318 C
six Hymns ending with	
ܐܕܡ ܣܝ ܠܣܘܢ.	V 325 F
ܐܬܘܬܐ ܡܢܝܢܬܐ. (3 Hymns)	V 327
ܨܒܝܬܐ ܐܘ ܐܡܪ.	V 330 F
ܐܠܗܐ ܒܗ ܘܠܒܗ.	V 336 D
ܒܢܘܗܝ ܚܕ ܐܚܪܢ.	V 338 F
ܠܡܠܟ ܕܥܡܢ ܘܣܓܕܐ.	V 344 B
ܠܘܩ ܚܘܣܐܝܢ ܠܕܢܝܐܝܠ.	V 350 D
ܗܐ ܚܣܢܐ ܥܡ ܗܕܝܘ.	V 359 D
ܘܟܣܡ ܐܝܟܘ ܥܠ ܟܠ ܚܛܝܐ.	V 387 B

De Nativitate Serm. XIII	V 396 —436
Sermones Polemici adversus Haereses LVI	V 437 ad fin.

---

[1] Extracted from the *Catena Patrum* made by one Severus of Edessa, AD 861.

B.O. vol. I	Cod. Vat. Syr.	B.M. Addit. (with the pp. of CBM)
I, p. 67	cx (vi°)	
I, p. 63	ciii (? ix°)	12144 (AD 1081), p. 908
I, p. 67	cx (vi°)	
I, p. 68 ff.	ciii (? ix°)	12144 (AD 1081), p. 908 ff.
	clii xv (AD 980)	
{IV 45—50, p. 91}	cxi 1 (AD 522)	14571 (AD 519), p. 411
IV 35—37, p. 90	cxi 1 (AD 522)	
X 7, p. 141	cxvii 73 (xii°)	
	(?)	17206 (xi°, xii°), p. 859
X 14, p. 146	cxvii 87 (xii°)	
X 15, p. 146	cxvii 89 (xii°) clv 27 (AD 1515)	14615 (x°, xi°), p. 840
X 16, p. 147	cxvii 88 (xii°)	17172 (AD 830), p. 761; 14611 (x°), p. 826; 7190 (xii°)
X 3, p. 140	cxvii 46 (xii°)	14573 (vi°), p. 413
X 20, p. 147	cxvii 153 (xii°)	17158 (vi°, vii°), p. 682 [*Jacob of Serug*]
II, pp. 80—84	cxii 2 (AD 551)	14571 (AD 519), p. 411
VII, pp. 118—132	cxi 4 (AD 522)	

S. EPHRAIM'S QUOTATIONS.

Title, or First Line.		Edit. Rom.
De Fide, adversus Scrutatores Hymni LXXXVII		VI 1 —164 C

Item de Fide (VI 164 D—208)

ܒܪܝܫܝܬܘܗܝ ܗܘܐ ܐܝܟ.	VI 164 D
ܪܒ ܗܘ ܐܝܟ ܕܡ ܕܐܠܗܐܘ.	VI 191 B
ܒܕ ܡܢܘ ܗܘ ܥܠܘܗܝ.	VI 195 C

Adversus Iudaeos

ܠܚܬܐܬܐ ܕܠܗ ܦܘܪܫܐ.	VI 209

Necrosima, Canones LXXXV — VI 225 —359

De Libero Voluntatis Arbitrio

ܐܝܟ ܕܒܠܝܐ ܪܘܗܝ.	VI 359 A
ܟܠܘܢ ܕܚܣܝܢܐ. ܕܗܡ ܐܝܟܘ	VI 362 A
[ܐܠܗܐ]¹ ܐܟܣܘܢ ܕܐܝܬܝ ܠܝ.	VI 364
ܐܝܟܘܢ ܕܗܒܝܬ ܗܘܐ.	VI 365 C

Paraenetica (VI 367—651)

ܡܚܝܒ ܩܒܝܠ ܒܕ ܠܥܘܠ.	I.	VI 367 A
ܠܚܝ ܝܕܗܘ ܐܝܟ.	II.	VI 369 C
ܠܐ ܐܝ ܕܒܐ ܕܗܘܐ.	III.	VI 379 B
ܐܘܗܐ ܐܝܕ ܕܐܝܟܐ ܗܘܐ.	IV.	VI 387 F

¹ ܐܠܗܐ is omitted in B.M. Add. 14574.

B.O. vol. I	Cod. Vat. Syr.	B.M. Addit. (with the pp. of CBM)
VI, pp 98—118	cxi 3 (AD 522) cxiii (vi°)	12176 (v°, vi°), p. 410
X 22, p. 147	cxvii 191 (xii°)	
,, 23	cxvii 192 (xii°)	
,, 24	cxvii 193 (xii°)	
X 21, p. 147	cxvii 154 (xii°) cxviii 50 (x°)	12165 (AD 1015), p. 847
VIII, pp. 132—138	I have not tried to trace out the MS sources of these Funeral Hymns. Many of those that are genuine are excerpts arranged for liturgical use (Bickell, *Carm. Nisibena*, § 2). They contain no quotations which imply the use of the Peshitta.	
IV 8, p. 87	cxi 1 (AD 522)	14571 (AD 519), p. 412
,, 9	,,	,,
,, 19	,,	14574 (vi°), p. 409
,, 12	,,	
IV 34, p. 90	cxi 1 (AD 522)	
X 12, p. 146	cxvii 81 (xii°)	
,, 13	cxvii 82 (xii°)	
[p. 233] no. 93	cxvii 190 (xii°) [ascr. to Isaac of Antioch in mg.]	

	Title, or First Line.		Edit. Rom.
Paraenetica]	.	V.	VI 412 D
	.	VI.	VI 415 C
	¹ .	VII.	VI 417
	.	VIII.	VI 420 E
	.	IX.	VI 422
	.	X.	VI 425
	.	XI.	VI 428 D
	.	XII.	VI 430 C
	.	XIII.	VI 431
	.	XIV.	VI 434 D
	.	XV.	VI 437 C
	.	XVI.	VI 438 E
	.	XVII.	VI 440 F
		XVIII.	VI 443 E
	.	XIX.	VI 447 E
	² .	XX.	VI 450 D
	.	XXI.	VI 451 F
	³ .	XXII.	VI 453 E
	.	XXIII.	VI 456
	⁴ .	XXIV.	VI 460 D

¹ For , 17173 has and 14592 has (*sic*).
² For , Ed. Rom. has against the *Bibliotheca Orientalis* ²/₂.
³ For Ed. Rom. and Cod. Vat. Syr. xciii have   ⁴ 17141 omits .

B.O. vol. I	Cod. Vat. Syr.	B.M. Addit. (with the pp. of CBM)
{ IX 1—11 } {pp. 138, 139}	xciii 4 I (AD 823)	
,,	,, III	
,,	,, IV	14592 (vi°, vii°), p. 686 17173 (vii°), p. 728 [ascr. in both to Jacob of Serug]
,,	,, V	14592 (vi°, vii°), p. 686 17173 (vii°), p. 728 14623 (AD 823), p. 765 [ascr. in all to Jacob of Serug]
,,	,, VI	
,,	,, VII	
,,	,, VIII	
,,	,, IX	
,,	,, X	
,,	,, XI	17141 (viii°, ix°), p. 359
,,	,, XIII	17173 (vii°), p. 729 [Jacob of Serug]
	(?)	
IX 13, p. 139	,, XVI	
,, 15	,, XVIII	
,, 12	,, XV	
,, 14 {IV 23} {p. 89}	,, XVII cxi 1 (AD 522) xciii 4 XII (AD 823)	17141 (viii°, ix°), p. 359
{IX ad fin.} { p. 139 }	,, II cxx 22 (vii°) [Isaac of Antioch]	14612 (vi°, vii°), p. 697 [Anon.[1]] 14728 (xiii°), p. 884 [Anonymous] 17141 (viii°, ix°), p. 360

[1] Ascribed to Ephraim in the margin by a hand not earlier than the 13th cent.

S. EPHRAIM'S QUOTATIONS.

	Title, or First Line.		Edit. Rom.
Paraenetica]	.	XXV.	VI 463 c
	.	XXVI.	VI 466 c
		XXVII.	VI 469
	.	XXVIII.	VI 473 c
		XXIX.	VI 476 d
	.	XXX.	VI 480 d
	.	XXXI.	VI 481 c
		XXXII.	VI 484 e
		XXXIII.	VI 485 d
		XXXIV.	VI 486 e
	[1] .	XXXV.	VI 488 b
	.	XXXVI.	VI 491
		XXXVII.	VI 492
		XXXVIII.	VI 493 c
	.	XXXIX.	VI 497
		XL.	VI 497 f
	.	XLI.	VI 499 b
		XLII.	VI 500 d
	.	XLIII.	VI 502 c
	.	XLIV.	VI 504 b
		XLV.	VI 505 e
	.	XLVI.	VI 507 f

[1] Ed. Rom.

B.O. vol. 1	Cod. Vat. Syr.	B.M. Addit. (with the pp. of CBM)
	xi 8 (AD 1261)	14728 (xiii°), p. 882
		7156 (xvii°)
		14677 (xiii°), p. 132
		17219 (xiii°), p. 134 [Narsa

* Those marked with this sign are in the Maronite Ferial Offices.

	Title, or First Line.		Edit. Rom.
Paraenetica]		XLVII.	VI 509 D
		XLVIII.	VI 511 C
		XLIX.	VI 512 F
		L.	VI 515
		LI.	VI 516 A
	.	LII.	VI 517
	.	LIII.	VI 517 F
	.	LIV.	VI 519 B
	.	LV.	VI 520
	.	LVI.	VI 520 F
	.	LVII.	VI 522 C
	.	LVIII.	VI 525 B
	.	LIX.	VI 526
		LX.	VI 527
		LXI.	VI 528 C
	.	LXII.	VI 532 B
	.	LXIII.	VI 533 C
	.	LXIV.	VI 534 D
	.	LXV.	VI 535 E
	.	LXVI.	VI 536 E

INDEX TO THE ROMAN EDITION. 15

B.O. vol. I	Cod. Vat. Syr.	B.M. Addit. (with the pp. of CBM)

*

*

*   7156 (xvii°)
                                        14675 (xiii°), p 131 [*Babai of*
*   17219 (xiii°), p. 136   *Nisibis*]

*

x 28, p. 149   (cod. Urb.)

x 29, p. 149   (cod. Urb.)

*

* (*cf* B.O. III¹ 149)   7156 (xvii°)
                                       14675 (xiii°), p. 131 [*George of*
                                       17219 (xiii°), p. 136   *Nisibis*]
*   7156 (xvii°)
                                       17219 (xiii°), p. 135
*   [*John of Beth Rabban*]

*

*   7156 (xvii°)
                                       14675 (xiii°), p. 130
                                       17219 (xiii°), p. 135

* Those marked with this sign are in the Maronite Ferial Offices.

	Title, or First Line.		Edit. Rom.
Paraenetica]	ܐܘ ܠܟܝ ܢܦܫܐ ܕܕܟܝܬ ܒܟܠܐ.	LXVII.	VI 537 C
	ܢܘܗܪܐ ܪܒܐ ܡܢܝ ܠܟܠܠܗ.	LXVIII.	VI 538 D
	ܐܘ ܠܟܝ ܢܦܫܐ ܕܒܛܠܬ ܒܟܠܐ.	LXIX.	VI 539 D
	ܡܪܝ ܢܦܩ ܡܠܟܐ ܡܫܝܚܐ.	LXX.	VI 540 E
	ܐܬܬܐ ܚܛܝܬܐ ܠܟ ܬܫܒܘ̄.	LXXI.	VI 541 F
	ܐܝܬ ܗܘ ܒܪܝܬܐ ܡܢ ܫܘܪܝܐ.	LXXII.	VI 543
	ܐܡܠܟ ܡܘܬܐ ܡܢ ܫܘܪܝܐ.	LXXIII.	VI 544 C
	ܢܦܩ ܫܘܦܪܐ ܕܒܡܘܬܐ:	LXXIV.	VI 545 D
	ܐܝܟ ܐܘܡܢ ܐܘ ܫܦܝܐ ܘܡܕܝܢܐ	LXXV.	VI 555 F
	ܒܦܪܐ ܗܝ ܡܪܝ ܬܪܒܝܬܝ ܡܢ	LXXVI.	VI 557 F

De Paradiso Eden, Sermones XII — VI 562—598

De Diversis Sermones (VI 599 *ad fin.*)

ܠܒܪܐ ܒܠܚܐ ܕܐܫܬܠܚ ܠܬܫܒܘ̄.	I.	VI 599
ܛܘܒ ܠܐܢܫܐ ܕܢܦܩ ܗܘܐ ܘܬܗܪ	II.	VI 603
ܬܗܪܐ ܪܒܐ ܫܡܥܝܢ.	III.	VI 604 F
ܐܫܡܥ ܡܪܝ ܡܢ ܡܟܘܒܝܢ.	IV.	VI 608 C
ܒܫܪܝܢ ܢܦܩ ܐܫܬܒܗܪ.	V.	VI 610 E
ܫܘܒܚܐ ܠܒܐܝܘܬܟ.	VI.	VI 613
ܬܒܒܗܝ[1] ܕܝܢ ܕܦܪܩܘ ܟ̈ܠܗ ܥܒ̈ܕܝ.	VII.	VI 615 B
ܐܠܗܐ ܗܘ ܕܒܬܪܗ ܒܦܘܪܫܢܗܝ.	VIII.	VI 618 F

[1] ܬܒܒܗܘ 14574.

INDEX TO THE ROMAN EDITION. 17

B.O. vol. I	Cod. Vat. Syr.	B.M. Addit. (with the pp. of CBM)
*		
*		
*		7156 (xvii°)
*		17219 (xiii°), p. 135
*		
*		
x 18, p. 147	cxvii 94 (xii°)	14607 (vi°, vii°), p. 685 [*Isaac of Antioch*]
IV 29, p. 89	cxi 1 (AD 522)	14571 (AD 519), p. 412 14574 (v°, vi°), p. 409
IV 30, p. 89	cxi 1 (AD 522)	14571 (AD 519), p. 412 14574 (v°, vi°), p. 409
{ III pp. 84, 85 }	cxi 5 (AD 522) cxii 1 (AD 551)	14571 (AD 519), p. 412
	(?)	[*cf Lamy* ii 821]
IV 51, p. 92	cxi 1 (AD 522)	
x 2, p. 140	cxvii 24 (xii°)	
IV 26, p. 89	cxi 1 (AD 522)	14571 (AD 519), p. 412 14574 (v°, vi°), p. 409
IV 27, p. 89	,,	14571 (AD 519), p. 412 14574 (v°, vi°), p. 409
IV 11, p. 87	,,	
IV 25, p. 89	,,	14571 (AD 519), p. 412 14574 (v°, vi°), p. 408
IV 52, p. 92	,,	

* Those marked with this sign are in the Maronite Ferial Offices.

B G. Q.

	Title, or First Line.		Edit. Rom.
[De Diversis Sermones]	ܐܘ ܠܟܐ ܕܠܗܐ ܠܟܠܒܐ.	IX.	VI 620 E
	ܣܘܢ ܠܟܠ ܠܫܡܥܬܐ.	X.	VI 622 E
	ܐܬܐ ܐܚܐ ܕܐܝܟ ܐܢܐ ܠܘܬܐܘܚܝ.	XI.	VI 624 E
	ܐܥܒܪ ܕܘܬܐ ܕܗܝܐ ܠܟ.	XII.	VI 627 E
	ܐܚ ܫܡܥܐ ܕܠܘܬܗ ܕܡܫܝܚܐ.	XIII.	VI 629 C
	ܡܢ ܐܕܡ ܠܡ ܐܬܟ ܕܢܫܐܠ.	XIV.	VI 638 F
	ܐܚܝ ܐܠ ܢܗܐ ܠܟ ܐܠܗܐ.	XV.	VI 644
	ܐܥܗܕܘ ܥܡ ܠܒܗ.	XVI.	VI 650 E
	ܐܫܡܥ ܕܚܟܡܬܐ ܐܥܒܕܘܢ.	XVII.	VI 652
	ܐܚܝ ܕܢܒܝ ܢܕܝܕ ܗܘ ܩܗ.	XVIII.	VI 654 F

[The first of the collection of miscellaneous homilies, called in the Edition *De Diversis Sermones*, is very likely to be genuine, as the first line is cited for the metre in a Hymn published by Lamy. But I have not been able to identify the Vatican MS from which it was edited in the Roman Edition.

INDEX TO THE ROMAN EDITION.

B.O. vol. I.	Cod. Vat. Syr.	B.M. Addit. (with the pp. of CBM)
IV 31, p. 89	cxi 1 (AD 522)	14571 (AD 519), p. 412
IV 32, p. 89	,,	
IV 28, p. 89	,,	14571 (AD 519), p. 412 14574 (v°, vi°), p. 409
IV 33, p. 90	,,	
x 5, p. 141	cxvii 59 (xii°)	
x 6, p. 141	cxvii 71 (xii°)	
[p. 232] no. 85 x 27, p. 149	cxvii 116 (xii°) [*Isaac of Antioch*][1] cod. Urb.	17262 (xii°), p. 873
	(?)	
x 19, p. 147	cxvii 97 (xii°)	14573 (vi°), p. 413

[1] Ascribed to Ephraim in *cod. Urb.* 151 and in B.M. Add. 17262.

A more careful search in the Maronite Service Books would no doubt bring to light the exact sources from which were taken such of the *Paraenetica* as are not here marked with an asterisk. The MSS which ascribe certain of the *Paraenetica* to less known writers, such as Narsai and George of Nisibis, are Nestorian Psalters.]

The above list sufficiently shews the haphazard way in which the Roman Edition was put together. The very first Homily (v 316—318 B) is not S. Ephraim's work. It is a vigorous composition, edited as a Sermon on the text that 'God created man in His own image,' but its main purpose is to enumerate the parts of the human body as known to ancient medical science, and then to encourage the study of Greek authors, such as Galen and Hippocrates and above all Aristotle. It would need a great deal of external evidence to prove that this kind of discourse was produced by S. Ephraim, in whose view "Blessed is he that hath not tasted the gall of Greek philosophy" (Ed. Rom. vi 4 E). As a matter of fact it is only found in a MS dated AD 980, which is chiefly taken up with grammatical tracts by Jacob of Edessa.[1]

This Homily does not directly touch the question in hand; it contains no quotations at all from the Gospel. The real battle concerns the homilies taken from Cod. Vat. Syr. cxvii, a paper MS of the 12th century, written at Amba Bishoi (S. Pisoes) in the Nitrian Desert and containing a collection of Festal Homilies for the whole ecclesiastical year. The preface to the book speaks only of Jacob of Serug, the voluminous Syriac Hymn-writer of the 5th and 6th centuries, and the greater part of the Festal Homilies are accordingly ascribed to him. But about twenty are assigned to S. Ephraim, and have accordingly been published as his in the Roman Edition, either among the *Sermones Exegetici* or the *Paraenetica* or the *De Diversis Sermones*.[2] Some of these are certainly genuine and are found elsewhere in ancient MSS of Ephraim's works: such is the long epic (as it has been called by an over-zealous admirer) on Jonah, printed in Ed. Rom. v 359 D—387 A; and such again is the last of the sermons "De Diversis" at the end of Ed. Rom. vi. Both of these are also extant in B.M. Add. 14573, of the 6th century. But the evidence of ancient MSS in the British

---

[1] In this MS (Vat. Syr. clii), no. XIV is 'A discourse composed by a certain philosopher on the Seven Regions in S. Ephraim's metre' (ܕܡܐܡܪܐ ܕܣܡܗ ܚܕ ܦܝܠܣܘܦܐ ܥܠ ܫܒܥ ܐܩܠܝܡܐ ܒܡܐܡܪܐ ܕܐܦܪܝܡ); no. XV is our Homily, headed 'Item, a discourse of S. Ephraim on the Composition of Man' (ܬܘܒ ܡܐܡܪܐ ܕܐܦܪܝܡ ܥܠ ܪܘܟܒܐ ܕܒܪܢܫܐ). It seems to me quite conceivable that the scribe meant no more than that this discourse, like the previous one, was written in Ephraimitic metre.

[2] They are enumerated by J. S. Assemani in *B. O.* I 139—148.

SOURCES OF THE ROMAN EDITION. 21

Museum does not always support the statements of the scribe of Vat. Syr. cxvii. No. LXXIV of the *Paraenetica* (ܟܬܒܐ ܕܡܟܣ, Ed. Rom. vi 545 D—555 E) is the 94th Homily in Cod. cxvii. This Homily is also extant in B.M. Add. 14607, a MS of the 6th or 7th century, but there it is expressly assigned to Isaac of Antioch and is found in company with other works of his.[1] Similarly the last of the so-called *Sermones Exegetici* (ܦܘܫܩܐ ܣܘܟܠܐ, Ed. Rom. v 387 B—395) is the 153rd Homily in cod. cxvii, but in B.M. Add. 17158, of the 6th or 7th century, it is ascribed to Jacob of Serug.[2] Which is to be trusted, the ancient MSS of the pre-Mohammedan East, or the headings of a 12th century collection of miscellaneous sermons?

The only reason that these questions of authorship have not been settled long ago is that very few people trouble themselves whether a certain metrical Homily be the work of Ephraim of Edessa or of some other Syriac writer whose name is even more unfamiliar. But when it is realised that the date of the Peshitta N.T. may depend upon the authorship of the Homily the matter assumes a very different aspect. Isaac of Antioch flourished in the middle of the fifth century; it is no surprise that he should use the ordinary Syriac version, for we have MSS of that version still extant, written either during his lifetime or immediately after his death. Jacob of Serug lived half a century after Isaac of Antioch. S. Ephraim, on the other hand, died about AD 373; if his testimony could be alleged for the Peshitta its date would be carried up into the fourth century, into the times before Greek theology and Greek influence were predominant in the Syriac-speaking Church.

Now as a matter of fact the passages from the Roman Edition which have been brought forward to prove S. Ephraim's use of the Peshitta are nearly all taken either from the Severus Catena or from the Homilies preserved in Cod. Vat. Syr. cxvii, the 12th century MS of which I have been speaking. For instance, it is from one of these Homilies that Mr Woods quotes Lk xvii 21 (*Woods* 129, Ed. Rom. vi 550 B, F). This passage is one of the few places where the Peshitta and the 'Old Syriac' and the Diatessaron are all extant and all different. The Greek is ἡ βασιλεία τοῦ θεοῦ ἐντὸς ὑμῶν ἐστίν. But for

---
[1] Wright, *CBM* 683. The Homily is No. 91 in Bickell's Catalogue of S. Isaac's Works.   [2] Wright, *CBM* 682.

ἐντὸς ὑμῶν the Peshitta and the Homily have *within you* (ܠܓܘ ܡܢܟܘܢ), while both *S* and *C* of the Old Syriac have *among you* (ܒܝܢܬܟܘܢ), and the Diatessaron (*Moes.* 209, 210) has *in your heart*. Thus there can be no doubt that the quotation in the Homily is derived from the Peshitta text of the Gospels. But we have seen that the Homily is not Ephraim's and should be ascribed to Isaac of Antioch on the sufficient authority of the 6th century MS in the British Museum.[1]

It would of course be too much to expect that all the Homilies wrongly ascribed to S. Ephraim in Cod. Vat. Syr. cxvii should be found assigned to their rightful authors in extant MSS of the 6th century. Many of the pieces in Cod. cxvii are found in no other MS. One of these, no. 73 in the MS (*B.O.* I 141, no. 7), is printed in Ed. Rom. v 330 F—336 C. It contains no quotations from the Gospel, but it is notorious as the one and only Syriac writing claiming to be earlier than Jacob of Edessa in the 7th century, which quotes the Apocalypse.[2] I do not think that the unsupported testimony of our 12th century Egyptian-made collection of Festal Homilies ought to outweigh the silence of so many Syriac writers and the absence of the Apocalypse from the Syriac canon. Most of my readers will doubtless agree with me that this so-called *Sermo Exegeticus* has nothing whatever to do with S. Ephraim or his times.[3]

The Severus Catena, the other main source from which quotations out of the Peshitta N.T. have been fathered upon S. Ephraim, was made at Edessa in the year 861 AD. Many of the extracts taken from it and edited in the Roman Edition as Ephraim's are not S. Ephraim's work, while in other instances the Biblical quotations (as in most Catenas) represent rather the texts familiar to the compiler than those used by the writers from whom the extracts have been made.[4]

---

[1] Similarly the reference to Matt xii 22 in the same Homily (Ed. Rom. vi 553 F ܕܗܢܐ ܗܘ ܒܪ ܕܘܝܕ), not noticed by Mr Woods, is demonstrably derived from the Peshitta.

[2] *Woods* 118, 138. The composition of this Homily need not be later than the early years of the 6th century, as Dr Gwynn's text of the Apocalypse seems to have been made about 500 AD.

[3] It is not for me to complain that Dr Gwynn accepts without investigation the genuineness of this Homily (*Apocalypse*, p. ciii), seeing that I myself have done the same (*Early Christianity outside the Roman Empire*, p. 17 note).

[4] For a further discussion of this Catena, see *Appendix* III.

THE GENUINE WRITINGS OF S. EPHRAIM.

The elimination of spurious documents, though in the case of any criticism of S. Ephraim's writings a most necessary preliminary to the work, is not the work itself. The real task before us is to determine the Gospel text used by S. Ephraim, and the only way to do this is to examine the quotations and allusions in the works which are admittedly genuine. When this is done, and not till then, it may be convenient to take the doubtful works into consideration. With the knowledge of S. Ephraim's text and his methods of quotation, that we shall have gained from a study of the certainly genuine works, we shall be better able to judge whether the other writings have been correctly ascribed to him.

The following list of genuine works by S. Ephraim has been drawn up on the principle of admitting only those which are extant in MSS earlier than the Mohammedan invasions. A mechanical rule such as this no doubt excludes some genuine writings, but the list at least escapes the charge of having been constructed to suit a pre-determined critical theory.

The Commentary on the *Diatessaron*—an undoubtedly genuine work—has not been included, because it is only extant in an Armenian translation. Besides, we may regard this Commentary as being, so to speak, on its trial. We know that S. Ephraim wrote a Commentary on the Diatessaron, while on the other hand there is absolutely no evidence which even suggests that he wrote upon any of the separate Four Gospels It is therefore the Diatessaron, and not the Four Gospels, which we should naturally expect to find quoted in his genuine works. But Mr Woods (p. 115) goes so far as to say that very few of S. Ephraim's quotations accord with the text of the Diatessaron where they differ from the Peshitta! No more striking instance could be given of the result of trusting to uncritical editions in matters of textual criticism.

List of the Genuine Writings of S. Ephraim.

PROSE WRITINGS:

(1)	The Commentary on Genesis and Exodus[1]	*Ed. Rom.* iv 1—115, 194—235
(2)	The Homily on our Lord	*Lamy* i 145—274, ii pp. xxi—xxiii
(3)	The fragments of the Homily on Joh i 1	*Lamy* ii 511—516
(4)	The fragments of the Treatises addressed to Hypatius against False Doctrines[2]	*Overbeck* 21—73
(5)	On the Fear of God, or *De Misericordia Divina*	,, 105—112
(6)	Letter to the Monks in the Mountains	,, 113—131

METRICAL WORKS (including both "Hymns" and "Homilies"):

(1)	'*Sermones Exegetici*' on Adam, etc.	*Ed. Rom.*	v 318 C—330
(2)	,, on Jonah	,,	v 359 D—387 A
(3)	*De Nativitate* XIII (see below, no. 20)	,,	v 396—436
(4)	*Sermones Polemici* LVI	,,	v 437 *ad fin.*
(5)	*De Fide adv. Scrutatores* LXXXVII	,,	vi 1—164
(6)	*De Libero Voluntatis Arbitrio* IV	,,	vi 359 A—366
(7)	'*Paraenetica*,' no. I	,,	vi 367—369 B
(8)	,, no. XX	,,	vi 450 D—451 F
(9)	,, nos. LXXV, LXXVI	,,	vi 555 F—561
(10)	*De Paradiso Eden* (see below, no. 15)	,,	vi 562—598
(11)	'*De Diversis Sermones*,' no. II	,,	vi 603—604 E
(12)	,, no. IV—XII	,,	vi 608 C—629 B
(13)	,, no. XVIII	,,	vi 654 F *ad fin.*

---

[1] The text in the Roman Edition must of course be corrected by Pohlmann's collations (*Journ. of Theol. Studies* i 570).

[2] The *Commentarii* (ܩܘܡܢܛܪܝ), edited as Ephraim's by Overbeck, pp. 74—104, are intentionally omitted from this List: see *Appendix* III.

LIST OF THE GENUINE WORKS. 25

(14)	On Julian the Apostate	Overbeck	3—20
(15)	*De Paradiso Eden* (supplement to no. 10)	„	339—354
(16)	The *Carmina Nisibena* (see below, no. 19)	Bickell's Edition	
(17)	*Hymni Azymorum*	Lamy	i 567—636
(18)	„ *De Crucifixione*	„	i 637—714
(19)	*Sermo de Reprehensione* I[1]	„	ii 332—362
(20)	*Hymni de Nativitate* (supplement to no. 3)	„	ii 501—510
(21)	Hymns on Fasting, Virginity, etc.	„	ii 647—678, 685—694, 718—814
(22)	*Sermones Rogationum*, nos. III, V—X	Lamy	iii 37—44, 65—114
(23)	Hymns on the Confessors	„	iii 643—696
(24)	„ on Abraham Kidunaya and on Julian Saba	„	iii 741—936

This may not be a complete list of the genuine extant works of S. Ephraim, but there can be little doubt that all those which are included are genuine. Every one of them is attested by at least one MS not later than the 7th century, and several are found in two MSS of the 5th or 6th century. Together they make up a very considerable mass of writing, certainly enough to settle the question whether S. Ephraim used the Peshitta text of the Gospels. It is, to say the least, exceedingly improbable that works which are assigned in later MSS to S. Ephraim should, if genuine, present a different type of text in the Biblical quotations and allusions from that found in these 350 separate poems, not to speak of the many pages of prose.

[1] This discourse (ܐܠܐ ܐܟܪ ܐܢܪܐ ܐܠܐ) appears to me to be one of the missing numbers of the *Carmina Nisibena* (either xxii, xxiii, or xxiv). It deals with the abandonment of Nisibis to the Persians by Jovian in 363 A.D. The second *Sermo de Reprehensione* (Lamy ii 363—392) is not, as stated on col. 312, taken from a MS of the 5th or 6th century. It is written on the fly-leaves of B.M. Add. 12176 in a hand of about the 9th century. It contains no quotations from the N. T. The *Sermo de Magis* (Lamy ii 393—426) is attested by no MS earlier than the 9th century, for the part of B.M. Add. 14650 in which it is found is not (as Lamy states) of the 6th or 7th century, but is dated A.D. 895; see *Appendix* III.

3 *

List of quotations from the Gospel found in certainly genuine works.

S. MATTHEW.

chap.	iii 17 ‖	*Rom.* v 545 A, vi 16 C
„	v 39 ‖	*Nis.* 72^{124}
„	ix 17	*Rom.* v 538 C
„	xi 19 ‖	*Lamy* ii 747
„	xiv 28 ff.	*Ov.* 27
„	xv 27	*Rom.* vi 585 D, & see on Mk vii 28
„	xvi 2, 3	*see on* Lk xii 54—56
„	xvi 18	*Ov.* 352
„	xvi 19	*Lamy* i 267
„	xviii 12 f. ‖	*Ov.* 114
„	xviii 22	*Nis.* 72^{168}
„	xxi 3	*Rom.* iv 108, 109
„	xxi 40, 41	*Lamy* i 253
„	xxii 13	*Nis.* 84^{230}
„	xxiii 8	*Rom.* v 491 B
„	xxvi 13	*Lamy* i 257
„	xxvii 46	*Rom.* v 558 A

S. MARK.

chap.	iv 39	*Lamy* i 263
„	vii 28	*Lamy* i 163
„	vii 33	*Lamy* i 171
„	xii 42	*Nis.* 91^{36}

S. LUKE.

chap.	ii 30	*Lamy* i 259, 261
„	ii 34	*Lamy* i 267
„	ii 36	*Lamy* iii 813
„	iii 22	*see on* Matt iii 17
„	iv 29	*Lamy* i 613; *Nis.* 59^{305}
„	vi 29	*see on* Matt v 39
„	vii 14	*Nis.* 72^{180}
„	vii 34	*see on* Matt xi 19
„	vii 41—43	*Lamy* ii, p. xxii f.

FROM THE GOSPEL. 27

chap.	ix 62	*Or.* 127
„	xii 49	*Or.* 124, 126
„	xii 54—56	*Rom.* v 320 B
„	xiv 31	*Rom.* v 487 A
„	xv 4 f.	*see on* Matt xviii 12 f.
„	xvii 31, 32	*Or.* 127
„	xviii 13	*Or.* 28
„	xxii 43	*Lamy* i 233, 665; *Nis.* 59²⁹
„	xxiii 38	*Lamy* i 667
„	xxiii 43	*Lamy* i 667, 669

S. JOHN.

chap.	i ff.	*Rom.* vi 62 A, 63 B
„	i 1	*Lamy* ii 513
„	i 3 f.	*Lamy* ii 513, 515
„	i 3	*Rom.* iv 18 E
„	i 14	*Lamy* ii 743
„	iii 34	*Lamy* i 267
„	vi 52	*Rom.* vi 102 F
„	xii 2	*Lamy* i 255
„	xiii 5	*Lamy* i 657
„	xiv 23	*Lamy* i 273
„	xv 1	*Lamy* ii 359
„	xvi 11	*Rom.* iv 37 F
„	xvii 11	*Rom.* vi 122 C
„	xix 30	*Lamy* i 229
„	xx 24	*Rom.* vi 16 F

We may notice in passing the very small total number of Gospel quotations. Thus in the fifty-six *Sermones Polemici*, the text and translation of which occupy 123 folio pages in the Roman Edition, there are only five quotations from the Gospel: and this, though many of the discourses are concerned with Marcion and his followers. The prose Homily on our Lord in *Lamy* i 145—274 has thirteen quotations, not a large allowance for just 65 columns of Syriac in a quarto volume. We must therefore look with suspicion on documents claiming to be Ephraim's work, which are full of Biblical quotations.

Examination of S. Ephraim's Quotations

Matt iii 17, Mk i 11, Lk iii 22 = *Rom.* v 545 A, VI 16 c

ܗܘܝܘ ܒܪܝ ܘܐܦ ܚܒܝܒܝ. (v 545 A)

'*This is my son, yea my beloved.*'

ܗܘܝܘ ܒܪܝ ܘܚܒܝܒܝ. (VI 16 c)

This is my son and my beloved.

For ܘܚܒܝܒܝ ('and my beloved'), Pesh. has ܚܒܝܒܐ ('the beloved') in accordance with the Greek ὁ υἱός μου ὁ ἀγαπητός, but ܘܚܒܝܒܝ is the reading of *S C* in Matt iii 17 and of *S* in Lk iii 22, i.e. of syr. vt wherever it is extant.[1]

The evidence of Ephraim in v 545 is all the more striking, as the quotation forms a 7-syllable line (*hánau lam bér áφ ḥabbíβ*) ; ܘܚܒܝܒܝ has only two syllables and so could not stand, but Ephraim instead of using the Peshitta *ḥabbíβā*, which would have satisfied both sense and metre, preferred to expand ܘܚܒܝܒܝ into ܐܦ ܚܒܝܒܝ.

Matt v 39, Lk vi 29 = *Nis.* 72[124]

ܕܡܚܐ ܠܟ ܥܠ ܦܟܟ. ܐܚܪܢܐ ܦܩܥ ܐܘܫܛ ܠܗ.

'*He that smiteth thee on thy cheek, thine other cheek present to him.*'

A paraphrase, partly caused by metrical considerations, but omitting 'right' as an epithet to 'cheek,' in agreement with *S* and *C* against Pesh.

Matt ix 17 = *Rom.* v 538 c

ܠܐ ܣܝܡܝܢ ܚܡܪܐ ܚܕܬܐ ܒܙܩܐ ܕܒܠܝ.

They do not set new wine in bottles that have worn out.

Pesh. and *S* both have ܪܡܝܢ 'put' for ܣܝܡ 'set,' and ܕܒܠܝܬ for ܕܒܠܝ. Here again the second variant in Ephraim is due to the metre.

---

[1] See also Matt xii 18 *C*, xvii 5 *C*; Lk ix 35 *C*. In Mk ix 7 and Lk ix 35 *S* has other renderings, but never the ܚܒܝܒܐ of the Peshitta.

Matt xi 19, Lk vii 34 = *Lamy* ii 747

ܡܢ ܐܳܟ݂ܘܿܠܳܐ ܐܶܬ݂ܚܫܶܒ݂ ܐܳܟܽܘܿܠܳܐ .... ܡܢ ܪܰܘܳܝܳܐ ܐܶܬ݂ܚܫܶܒ ܫܳܬ݂ܶܐ.

By the dissipated He was thought an eater....by the drunkards He was thought a drinker.

The opprobrious words φάγος and οἰνοπότης seem to have offended the later translators, both in Syriac and Latin. φάγος of course could not be avoided; it means *uorax* and had to be so translated, while the Syriac equivalent is ܐܳܟܽܘܠܳܐ, literally 'an eater' but practically meaning 'glutton.' But οἰνοπότης could be softened by translating it etymologically. Accordingly the Latins used *bibens uinum* and *potator uini* to replace the older *uinaria* preserved in *k* and Augustine, while the Peshitta (followed by the Harclean) has ܫܳܬ݂ܶܐ ܚܰܡܪܳܐ 'drinking wine.' The scandal of calling our Lord a wine-bibber was thus avoided. But instead of ܫܳܬ݂ܶܐ ܚܰܡܪܳܐ we find ܪܰܘܳܝܳܐ 'a drunkard' in Lk vii 34 *S C*, and ܫܰܬܳܝܳܐ (*shattāyā*) i.e 'a drinker,' 'one given to drink,' in Matt xi 19 *S C*: this latter is the word used by Ephraim.

Matt xiv 28 ff. = *Overbeck* 27 : *cf also Lamy* i 263

This is a reference to the story of S. Peter walking on the water, textually interesting because he is twice called ܫܶܡܥܽܘܢ (ll. 7, 27) and only once ܟܺܐܦܳܐ (l. 18). The name comes twice in the narrative, and Pesh. has ܟܺܐܦܳܐ i.e. 'Cephas,' while *S* and *C* have 'Simon Cephas.' The Greek form 'Petros' is very uncommon in the Syriac text of the Gospels : it occurs only in such places as Joh i 42 *S*. In a somewhat similar allusion to the same story in *Lamy* i 263 the name Simon alone occurs.

Matt xv 27 = *Rom.* vi 585 D

This is best taken in connexion with the quotation of Mk vii 28.

Matt xvi 2, 3; see on Lk xii 54—56

Matt xvi 18   *Overbeck* 352

[Syriac text]

...*the word of our Lord, that of His Church He spake, that 'the gate-bars of Sheol shall not be able to conquer it.'*

The 'gate-bars of Sheol' (πύλαι ᾅδου) occur again in Eus. *Theoph*^syr iii 27, iv 11, v 40, and in *HE*^syr 417. The same graphic phrase is also found in a passage ascribed to Ephraim in the Severus Catena. In Matt xvi 18 *C* and Pesh. have [Syriac] 'the doors of Sheol': א is unfortunately not extant.

Matt xvi 19 = *Lamy* i 267

[Syriac text]

He said to Simon, 'To thee I will give the keys of the doors.'

The Peshitta has here, in accordance with the Greek, 'the keys of the kingdom of heaven,' but *C* has 'the keys of the doors of the kingdom of heaven.' Thus Ephraim's text agrees with *C* against Pesh. in an addition for which no other authority is known. א is deficient; Aphraates 141 has 'Hear ye also, that hold the keys of the doors of heaven.'

Matt xviii (12,) 13, Lk xv 4, (5)   *Overbeck* 114

[Syriac text]

FROM THE GOSPEL.

[Syriac text]

'Who is there of you that hath beasts in the hill-country, and one sheep stray from him,— doth he not leave the ninety and nine in the plain and in the hill, and come and seek that which strayed until he find it?'

'And what time he hath found it, he rejoiceth over it more than those ninety and nine that did not stray.'

It is difficult to believe that a mosaic such as this can have come from anywhere but the Diatessaron. There is nothing in the wording which definitely indicates the use either of the Peshitta text or of that found in S and C, except that [Syriac] as a rendering for πρόβατα occurs in Joh x 3 ff. in S, but never in the Peshitta. The Arabic Diatessaron (xxvi 4, 5) gives us Lk xv 4 followed by Matt xviii 13, which is practically what we find in Ephraim, but without the characteristic phrase [Syriac] which combines the ἐν τῇ ἐρήμῳ of Lk xv 4 with the ἐπὶ τὰ ὄρη of Matt xviii 12.

Matt xviii 22 = Nis. 72[iii]

[Syriac text]

Forgive thy brother (he saith) 'by sevens seventy times over.'

The idiomatic [Syriac] which is here used something like the English 'for' ('in batches of seven, for seventy times') is found in S C and Aphraates 35 and 298. And as if to remove all doubt as to the exact meaning the number is stated in Aphraates 298 to be 490 times. But the Peshitta, in more literal accordance with the Greek, has 'unto seventy times by sevens' ([Syriac]).[1]

---

[1] The addition of [Syriac] in Pesh. is not significant, as both S and A 2/3 add [Syriac] after [Syriac].

Matt xxi 3 = *Rom.* iv 108, 109 (*cf* Pohlmann ii 52, 54)

ܐܡܪܘ ܠܗܘܢ ܕܠܡܪܗܘܢ ܡܬܒܥܝܢ. (*sic* MS)

Say ye to them that for their Lord they are required.

So also *C* has ܠܡܪܗܘܢ ܡܬܒܥܝܢ for ὁ κύριος αὐτῶν χρείαν ἔχει.

This quotation, short as it is, presents several points of difficulty and interest. It comes from the Commentary on Genesis, an undoubtedly genuine prose work of S. Ephraim, and is assigned by Mr Woods to Mk xi 2, 3. The text of the quotation which Mr Woods had before him (Ed. Rom. iv 108, 109) runs thus :—

ܐܡܪ ܓܝܪ [ܡܫܟܚܝܢ ܐܢܬܘܢ ܥܝܠܐ ܕܐܣܝܪ. ܫܪܘ ܐܝܬܐܘܗܝ.]
ܕܐܢ ܐܡܪܝܢ ܠܟܘܢ ܡܢܐ ܫܪܝܢ ܐܢܬܘܢ ܥܝܠܐ ܗܘ. ܐܡܪܘ
ܠܗܘܢ ܕܠܡܪܢ ܡܬܒܥܐ.

For He said [*Ye will find a colt tied; loose him and bring him.*] *that if they say to you 'Why are ye loosing that colt?' say to them that for our Lord it is required.*

The brackets are my own insertion.

Mr Woods calls the quotation a combination of Mark and Matt., and notes that while *C* (the Curetonian) has many verbal variations from the Peshitta, yet in the only 'important variation' it differs from Ephraim's quotation where the quotation agrees with the Peshitta.

The 'important variation' concerns the words which in the Greek of Matt xxi 3 run

ὁ κύριος αὐτῶν χρείαν ἔχει

(Mk xi 3 and Lk xix 34 have of course αὐτοῦ in the singular). The extant Syriac readings are

1 'For our Lord they are (*or* it is) required' Pesh. (Matt.) (Mk., Lk.).

2*a* 'For their Lord they are required' *C* (Matt.).

2*b* 'For its Lord it is required' *S C* (Lk.) *S* (Mk.).[1]

It is evident that we have here two independent interpretations of the Greek. According to the Peshitta ὁ κύριος is used absolutely of Christ (as so often in Lk, so rarely in Matt and Mk) : according to *S*

[1] In Mk xi 3 *S* reads ܕܠܡܪܗ, as is clear from the photograph, not ܠܡܪܝܐ as edited. *S* is not extant for Matt xxi 3, and *C* is not extant for Mk xi 3.

and *C*, on the other hand, αὐτῶν or αὐτοῦ is taken with κύριος, so that it means the 'master' of the animals, either as Lord of all creatures or as their legal possessor.

Thus the quotation in S. Ephraim's Commentary on Genesis, as given in the Roman Edition, presents quite a striking agreement with the Peshitta. The passage printed above within brackets agrees verbally with clauses in the Peshitta text of Mk xi 2 and 3, and the last two words agree in a characteristic variation with the Peshitta against the MSS of the *Evangelion da-Mepharreshe*.

But the fact is that the text of the Roman Edition does not in the least represent the text of the MS upon which it is based. The MS (Vat. Syr. cx) was examined some time ago by Dr A. Pohlmann, who published a tract upon it in 1862—4. The practical result of this investigation is that you can never trust a Biblical quotation in the printed text of the Commentary where it verbally agrees with the Peshitta. In the present instance the bracketed passage is not in the MS at all, having been added *de suo* by the editor (Pohlmann, p. 52); while for the last two words the MS actually has (Pohlmann, p. 54)

in exact accordance with the Curetonian text of Matt xxi 3! The translation therefore of S. Ephraim's reference to the Entry into Jerusalem should run

'For He said that if they say to you 'Why are ye loosing that colt?' say to them that for their Lord¹ they are required.'

I may add that if the quotation was taken by S. Ephraim from the Diatessaron, as seems probable, it was only to be expected that it should give us the text of S. Matthew (who alone mentions two animals) rather than that of S. Mark and S. Luke.[2]

---

[1] Or, 'for their master.'

[2] This quotation of S. Ephraim was discussed by the present writer in the *Journal of Theological Studies* i 569 ff.

Matt xxi 40, 41 = *Lamy* i 253

ܡܢܐ ܠܡ ܓܝܪ ܢܥܒܕ ܡܪܐ ܕܟܪܡܐ ܠܗܢܘܢ ܦܠܚ̈ܐ.
41 ܐܡܪܝܢ ܠܗ ܕܝܢ ܗܢܘܢ ܥܠ ܢܦܫܗܘܢ ܕܒܝܫ ܒܝܫ
ܢܘܒܕ ܐܢܘܢ ܘܢܘܓܪ ܟܪܡܐ ܠܦܠܚ̈ܐ. ܐܝܠܝܢ ܕܡܣܩܝܢ
ܠܗ ܐܒܒܐ ܒܙܒܢܗ.

For 'What (quoth He) will the master of the vineyard do to those husbandmen?

[41] *But they say to him concerning themselves that evilly he will destroy them and will let out the vineyard to husbandmen which raise for him the produce in its season.'*

Two points deserve notice in this quotation, which comes from the prose Homily on our Lord. The only part of it which appears to be intended for a real quotation is the answer of the Pharisees: that this is a real quotation is certain from the occurrence in it of the peculiar Syriac rendering of Matt xxi 41.[1] But the final clause in Ephraim differs altogether both from the Syriac Vulgate and the *Evangelion da-Mepharreshe*. At the same time Ephraim's 'raise for him the produce' is as good a representation of ἀποδώσουσιν αὐτῷ τοὺς καρποὺς as 'give to him the fruits' (ܢܬܠܘܢ ܠܗ ܦܐܪ̈ܐ), which is the rendering found in *S C* and the Peshitta.

The other point concerns the rendering of ἐκδώσεται in Matt xxi 41. In ܢܘܓܪ 'he will let out (on hire)' Ephraim and Pesh. agree against *S C*. This word is used in all the Syriac texts of Mk xii 1 and Lk xx 9. But in the passage before us *S* has ܢܬܠ 'he will give' (as in Mk xii 9 and Lk xx 16), and *C* has ܢܫܠܡ 'he will deliver' (as in Matt xxi 33 *S C*). Thus the text of S. Matthew as given in *S* and *C* seems to avoid the word ܐܘܓܪ, though its occurrence in S. Mark and S. Luke

[1] The clause referred to is ܒܝܫ ܒܝܫ ܢܘܒܕ ܐܢܘܢ, which corresponds to κακοὺς κακῶς ἀπολέσει αὐτοὺς in *S C* and Pesh., as well as in the quotation of Ephraim. Judging by the phrase ܒܝܫ ܒܝܫ ܚܫܝܫܝܢ, which so often stands for κακῶς ἔχοντες, this rendering might be held to imply the omission of κακούς, but it is more likely to be nothing more than an attempt to give the effect of the alliteration in the Greek. *Moes*. 192 has 'malos per mala perdet' (զչարսն չարեօք սատակեսցէ), but this Armenian rendering may have been influenced by the Armenian vulgate which has զչարսն չարա...

shews that it was the natural one to use; it is therefore clear that S. Ephraim's quotation cannot be explained by the use of the *Evangelion da-Mepharreshe*. But neither can S. Ephraim's quotation be explained by the use of the Peshitta alone, as in the final clause the quotation differs as much from the diction of the Peshitta as from that of *S* and *C*. It may reasonably be conjectured that here as in other places S. Ephraim is giving us the text of the *Diatessaron*, and that the agreement in this single point between the Diatessaron as represented by Ephraim and the Syriac Vulgate is merely the result of literally rendering the Greek. But instances of this agreement are so rare compared with those where the renderings of the Diatessaron agree with the *Evangelion da-Mepharreshe* against the Syriac Vulgate that it is worth while to draw special attention to those which make the other way. The case is in every way similar to that of ܐܚܕ ܓܝܪ in Lk vii 43, to be discussed later on.

Matt xxii 13 = *Nis.* 84[230]

ܦܟܪܘܗܝ, ܠܗܘ ܕܦܓܪܗ. ܛܢܦ ܗܘܐ.

They fettered that man, whose body was defiled.

The reference to the Parable of the Wedding Feast is quite clear in the context, and S. Ephraim has just explained that the body is the wedding-garment, which ought to be kept bright and clean.

S. Ephraim obviously supports the reading of the better Greek MSS δήσαντες αὐτοῦ πόδας καὶ χεῖρας ἐκβάλετε αὐτόν...., which is also the reading of Pesh.; while *S* and *C* have 'Take hold of him by his hands and by his feet and put him forth,' which seems to represent ἄρατε αὐτὸν ποδῶν καὶ χειρῶν καὶ βάλετε αὐτόν..., the reading of D and lat.vt. But whereas Pesh. here uses the ordinary word ܐܣܪ for 'bind,' Ephraim has ܦܟܪ to 'fasten' or 'fetter,' a word which only occurs once in the N.T. Peshitta, *viz.* Ac xxii 29. It might naturally be thought that Ephraim's use of ܦܟܪ was a mere paraphrastic alteration of the Biblical text, but the same word occurs in the quotation of Matt xxii 13 in the Syriac Theophania iv 16, and in an express allusion in the Syriac *Acts of Thomas* (Wright, p. 315). A version of this passage, therefore, containing the word ܦܟܪ instead of ܐܣܪ, must have been once current, and from this version and not from the Peshitta was S. Ephraim's quotation made. It is unfortunate that no allusion to Matt xxii 13 is made in the Commentary on the *Diatessaron*.

Matt xxiii 8 = *Rom.* v 491 B

ܪܒܐ ܒܐܪܥܐ ܠܐ ܬܩܪܘܢ܀

Ye shall not call (any one) a great one on earth.

This agrees with *S C*, which have ܐܢܬܘܢ ܕܝܢ ܠܐ ܬܩܪܘܢ ܪܒܝ i.e. 'but ye, ye shall not call (any one) Rabbi'; Pesh., on the other hand, has ܬܬܩܪܘܢ instead of ܬܩܪܘܢ, making the sense to be 'but ye, ye shall not be called Rabbi,' in accordance with the Greek.

Matt xxvi 13 = *Lamy* i 257

ܢܗܘܐ ܠܗ̇ ܐܡܪ ܫܡܐ ܘܗܢܐ ܕܘܟܪܢܐ. ܒܟܠ ܐܬܪ
ܕܡܬܟܪܙ ܣܒܪܬܝ.

For 'There shall be to her (quoth He) a name and this memorial everywhere that my Gospel shall be announced.'

There is no trace of this recasting of the verse either in the Peshitta or in the *Evangelion da-Mepharreshe*, so that it is possible that Ephraim's words are a conscious paraphrase.[1]

Matt xxvii 46 = *Rom.* v 558 A

ܐܝܠ ܐܝܠ ܠܡܢܐ ܫܒܩܬܢܝ. (*sic*)

Eli, El, why hast thou left me?

For the first words *S* has ܐܝܠ ܐܝܠ (i.e. 'Eli, Eli') in Matt. and ܐܠܗܝ ܐܠܗܝ (i e. 'My God, my God') in Mk. Pesh. has ܐܝܠ ܐܝܠ both in Matt. and in Mk. I owe the correct transcription of Cod. Vat. Syr. cxi (p. 263 *a*), given above, to the kindness of Dr G. Mercati, of the Vatican Library.

[1] ܗܢܐ (i.e. 'this') is omitted in B.M. Add. 14654.

Mark iv 39 = *Lamy* i 263

ܫܠܝ ܠܟ ܐܝܬ ܣܟܡܝܕܝ.

For '*Be quiet!* (*quoth He*) *thou art muzzled!*'
B.M. Add. 14654 (Lamy's B, but not cited by him here) has
ܫܠܝ ܠܟ ܐܢܬ ܫܠܝ 'Be quiet! thou art stilled!' But both the MSS of
S. Ephraim's Homily agree in having a feminine participle, so that
the rebuke is addressed to the wind. *S* and *C* are unfortunately both
missing, but Pesh. has ܫܠܝ ܠܟ ܐܝܟ (with masc. verbs and pronoun),
and the rebuke is addressed to the sea. Here again therefore
S. Ephraim shews his independence of the Peshitta.

Mark vii 28 (Matt xv 27) = *Lamy* i 163 (*cf Rom.* VI 585 D)

ܕܬܣܒܥ ܐܢܘܢ ܡܢ ܦܪܬܘܬܐ ܕܡܢ ܦܬܘܪܐ ܕܒܢܝܐ
ܢܦܠܝܢ. ܗܘܘ.

*That thou shouldest satisfy them from the crumbs that from the sons'
table were falling.*

(*Rom.* VI 585 D has

ܟܠܒܐ ܡܢ ܦܪܬܘܬܐ ܕܡܪܝܗܘܢ ܣܒܥܝܢ.

Dogs from the crumbs of their masters are satisfied.)
The second quotation occurs in the Hymns *De Paradiso* and is
obviously a paraphrase. It is however noteworthy that both quotations
agree in having a form of the verb ܣܒܥ 'satisfy.' The first quotation
is from the prose Homily on our Lord, and is remarkable for containing
the phrase "the sons' table," which is not found in any Greek MS or
in the Peshitta, but does actually occur in Mk vii 28 according to *S*
and arm. vg. That it was also the reading of the Diatessaron is
probable from *Moes.* 138, where Moesinger's cod. B has "Yea, Lord,
even dogs eat of the crumbs of the children's table."[1] Here again
therefore Ephraim, the *Evangelion da-Mepharreshe* and the Diatessaron

---

[1] The other MS has "their masters' table," in agreement with Matt xv 27.

unite in preserving a singular expression, of which the Peshitta has no trace¹.

The allusion in *Rom.* VI 585 D to this saying of Christ is chiefly remarkable for the word ܪ̈ܥܦܐ 'crumbs.' This word is synonymous in meaning with the word ܦܪܬܘܬܐ used in syr. vt-vg, and is also metrically equivalent. The fact that it is found in the Harclean (both in Matt xv 27 and Mk vii 28) is curious, but the circumstance is too isolated to have any special significance.

Mark vii 33 = *Lamy* i 171

ܐܡ ܠܗ ܨ̈ܒܥܬܗ ܣܡ ܒܐ̈ܕܢܘܗܝ, ܕܗܘ ܚܪܫܐ.

'*He spat on his fingers and put (it) in the ears of that deaf-mute.*'

The variants in Mk vii 33 are particularly interesting: there are four rival readings extant in Greek, and three of these (if not all four) are represented in Syriac, or in translations from the Syriac.

(a) ܐܪܡܝ ܨ̈ܒܥܬܗ ܒܐ̈ܕܢܘܗܝ ܘܪܩ ܘܩܪܒ ܠܠܫܢܗ Pesh.

He laid his fingers in his ears, and spat and touched his tongue.

This is the reading supported by most Greek MSS, including B (ℵ) and the 'Received Text' (ἔβαλεν τοὺς δακτύλους αὐτοῦ εἰς τὰ ὦτα αὐτοῦ καὶ πτύσας ἥψατο τῆς γλώσσης αὐτοῦ).

(b) ܣܡ ܨ̈ܒܥܬܗ ܘܪܩ ܒܐ̈ܕܢܘܗܝ ܘܩܪܒ ܠܠܫܢܗ S

He put his fingers and spat in his ears and touched his tongue.

This is the reading of the 'Ferrar Group' and of the very important minuscule 28 ([ἐπ]έβαλεν τοὺς δακτύλους αὐτοῦ πτύσας εἰς τὰ ὦτα αὐτοῦ καὶ ἥψατο τῆς γλώσσης αὐτοῦ).

---

¹ The actual texts found in Syr. vt-vg are:—

ܐܦ ܟܠܒܐ ܐܟܠܝܢ ܡܢ ܦܪܬܘܬܐ ܕܢܦܠܝܢ ܡܢ ܦܬܘܪܐ ܕܡܪ̈ܝܗܘܢ.
Mk vii 28 S

ܐܦ ܟܠܒܐ ܡܢ ܬܚܝܬ ܦܬܘܪܐ ܐܟܠܝܢ ܦܪܬܘܬܐ ܕܛܠܝ̈ܐ.
Mk vii 28 Pesh.

ܐܦ ܟܠܒܐ ܐܟܠܝܢ [ܡܢ] ܦܪܬܘܬܐ [ܕܢܦܠܐ ܡܢ] ܦܬܘܪܐ ܕܡܪ̈ܝܗܘܢ ܘܚܐܝܢ
Matt xv 27 Pesh. (S) (C)

[S omits the bracketed words, C adds ܠܗܘܢ after ܦܬܘܪܐ].

(*c*) نفث علي اصابعه والقي في اذنيه ولمس لسانه Diat^ar xxi 3

He spat on his fingers and put (it) in his ears and touched his tongue.

This agrees with Ephraim's quotation, and is attested in Greek by the uncial fragment called W^d (ἐπτυσεν εἰς τουσ δακτύλουσ αὐτοῦ· και εβαλεν εἰσ τὰ ὦτα τοῦ κωφοῦ · καὶ ἥψατο τῆσ γλωσσασ του μογγιλάλου). The passage is not quoted in Ephraim's Commentary, but the fact that the Arabic Diatessaron does not agree with the Peshitta makes it certain that the Arabic has here preserved the ancient Syriac text substantially unaltered.[1]

In this passage, therefore, Ephraim follows the transmitted text of the Diatessaron, while both the Peshitta and the *Evangelion da-Mepharreshe* differ from it and from each other.

Mark xii 42 = *Nis.* 91^36f.

ܠܡܢܝܗ̇ ܘܫܡܘܢܐ ܐܘܪܒܗ ܕܐܪܡܠܬܐ.

The pound and the mite of the widow he increased.

S has ܬܪ̈ܬܝܢ ܫܡܘܢܝܢ ܕܐܝܬܝܗܘܢ ܪܘܒܥܐ 'two mites which are a quarter' for λεπτὰ δύο, ὅ ἐστιν κοδράντης. But the Peshitta has ܬܪ̈ܬܝܢ ܡ̈ܢܝܢ ܕܐܝܬܝܗܘܢ ܫܡܘܢܐ 'two pounds which are mites.' This is obviously the rendering followed by S. Ephraim.

It seems to me very probable that in this case as in many others the Peshitta has retained unaltered a previously existing Syriac rendering. For it is wholly unfair to equate the μνᾶ (*Mina* or *Maneh*) of the Parable of the Pounds with the λεπτὸν of the poor widow, and the later Syriac scholars were quite incapable of originating such a mistake.[2] My friend Professor A. A. Bevan suggests that the original

[1] The fourth reading, found in D (2^pe) lat. vt, puts πτύσας before ἔβαλεν, but otherwise agrees with (*a*). By a curious coincidence this reading is found in the Discourses of Philoxenus (*Budge* i 45). His words are

ܪܡܐ ܘܩܪܒ ܬܪ̈ܬܝܗ ܒܐܕ̈ܢܘܗܝ ܕܗܘ ܚܪܫܐ

which looks like a conflation of the *Evangelion da-Mepharreshe* with the Diatessaron, as Philoxenus can hardly have derived his text direct from D and the Latins.

[2] The Harclean has ܠܦܛܐ, i.e. the Greek word transliterated.

rendering may have been ܩܣܡ, in which case we must read ܐܬܝܕܗ and ܕܡܣܒܪ, as ܡܣܒ (a small coin, Heb. *gera*) is feminine.[1]

Luke ii 30 = *Lamy* i 259, 261

ܗܐ ܓܝܪ ܚܙܝ, ܥܝܢܝ ܚܢܢܟ.

'*Lo, mine eyes have seen thy Mercy!*'

This agrees both with *S* and the Peshitta. The regular equivalent for τὸ σωτήριόν σου, according to Syriac Biblical usage, would be ܚܝܝܟ 'thy Life,' and ܚܢܢܟ 'thy Mercy' looks like an intentional alteration of this. But if so, the alteration must have taken place before S. Ephraim's day.

Luke ii 34 = *Lamy* i 267

ܗܢܐ ܣܝܡ ܗܘ ܠܡܦܘܠܬܐ ܘܠܩܝܡܬܐ.

'*This one is set for falling and for rising.*'

The same words (and no more) are quoted in a passage of the Severus Catena (*Rom.* IV 129, 130), on which Mr Woods remarks: "The use of this expression without any further limitation is certainly curious. Now in the translation of the Commentary on the Diatessaron (see Zahn, II. ii. §4 [*Moesinger* 28]) we have *Ecce hic stat in ruinam et in resurrectionem et in signum contradictionis*, and Ephrem's comment shows that this is not an abbreviation but a real variant. It seems likely therefore that we have in this quotation an omission of the words 'of many in Israel' influenced by the Diatessaron." Mr Woods's argument is certainly strengthened by the passage quoted above from the undoubtedly genuine *Homily on our Lord*. In this verse, the Peshitta has the ordinary text 'This one is set for the falling and for the rising of many in Israel'; but *S* presents us with the curious order 'This one is set in Israel for the falling and for the rising of many.'

[1] The very same corruption also occurs in the Jerusalem Targum to Exod xxx 13, which has מני where Onkelos has מעין.

Luke ii 36 = *Lamy* iii 813

ܕܟܡܐ ܕܕܡܝܐ ܢܟܦܐ. ܠܢܟܦܬ ܢܟܦܐ. ܕܗܘܬ ܥܡ ܒܥܠܐ ܫܒܥܐ ܝܘܡܝܢ.

How like is the modest one (i.e. Julian Saba, who deserted his wife) *to that most modest of the modest, who 'for seven days had been with a husband.'*

According to the Peshitta, as in the ordinary text, Hanna the prophetess had lived seven *years* with a husband, but *S* alone among MSS and versions makes it into seven *days* only, and in so doing is followed by Ephraim.

Luke iii 22 ; see on Matt iii 17

Luke iv 29 = *Nis.* 59[205], *Lamy* i 613

ܟܕ ܫܕܐܘܗܝ, ܡܢ ܛܘܪܐ. ܦܪܚ ܒܐܐܪ ܠܗ ܐܬܪܐ. (*Nis.*)

When they threw him from the hill, he flew in the air.

ܟܕ ܬܘܒ ܫܕܐܘܗܝ, ܡܢ ܪܝܫ ܛܘܪܐ. (*Lamy*)

When again they threw him from the top of the hill...

It is clear from these phrases that S. Ephraim used a text which represented ὥστε κατακρημνίσαι αὐτόν, and took these words to imply that the people of Nazareth actually threw our Lord over the cliff. This is also the view taken in the Commentary on the Diatessaron *Moes.* 130, 212), which no doubt represents the text as read in Tatian's Harmony. But it is not supported either by *S* or the Peshitta. *S* has 'so that they might hang him' (i.e. ὥστε [κατα]κρεμάσαι αὐτόν), while the Peshitta has 'that they might throw him from the cliff' (i.e. εἰς τὸ κατακρημνίσαι αὐτόν, the reading of the 'Received Text').

Luke vi 29; see on Matt v 39

Luke vii 14 = *Nis.* 72[179, 180]

ܩܥܐ ܕܝܢ ܝܫܘܥ ܠܡܝܬܐ. ܛܠܝܐ ܛܠܝܐ.

Now Jesus called to the dead man 'Youth, youth!'

This remarkable reading is expressly attested by Aphraates, who says (p. 165): "And with two words He raised each one of them. For the son of the widow, when He raised him, He called twice, saying to him 'Youth, youth, arise!'—and he lived and arose. And the daughter of the chief of the Synagogue He called twice, saying to her 'Girl, girl, arise!'[1]—and her spirit returned and she arose." Thus Ephraim's reading (which is also that of D and of *a ff* of the Old Latin), was that which was alone familiar to Aphraates, and we may safely conjecture that it stood in the Diatessaron. But it is not the reading either of the Peshitta or of *S*.

Luke vii 34; see on Matt xi 19

Luke vii 41—43 = *Lamy* ii, p. xxii f. (*supplying the lacuna in* i 249)

41 ܬܪܝܢ ܠܗ ܚܝܒܝܢ ܐܝܬ ܗܘܘ ܠܓܒܪܐ ܡܘܙܦܢܐ. ܚܕ ܠܗ
ܚܝܒ ܗܘܐ ܕܝܢܪܐ ܚܡܫܡܐܐ ܘܐܚܪܢܐ ܕܝܢ ܕܝܢܪܐ
ܚܡܫܝܢ. ܡܟܝܠ ܠܗ 42 ܟܕ ܠܝܬ ܠܚܕ ܡܢܗܘܢ ܕܢܦܪܥܝܘܗܝ،
ܠܬܪܝܗܘܢ ܫܒܩ. ܠܐܝܢܐ ܡܟܝܠ ܐܢܬ ܣܐܡ ܒܪܥܝܢܟ ܕܝܬܝܪ
ܢܚܒܝܘܗܝ. 43 ܐܡܪ ܠܗ ܫܡܥܘܢ ܣܒܪ ܐܢܐ ܕܗܘ
ܕܐܫܬܒܩ ܠܗ ܣܓܝ. ܐܡܪ ܠܗ ܡܪܢ ܬܪܝܨܐܝܬ ܕܢܬ.

41 '*Two debtors there were to a man, a money-lender. One was in debt for five hundred denars, but the other for fifty denars.*' '*Finally,* 42 *when not one of them had aught to pay him, he forgave them both. Which dost thou set in thy mind will most love him?*' 43 *Simon saith to him 'I suppose it is he to whom he forgave much.' Our Lord saith to him 'Correctly hast thou judged.'*

[1] Or we may regard it as a transliteration and render it '*Talitha, talitha, cumi.*' Traces of this reading also are to be found in D and the Latin texts of Mk v 41.

FROM THE GOSPEL. 43

It will not be necessary to give in full all the trifling variations between Ephraim's not absolutely accurate quotation and the Biblical MSS. The three significant readings are: (1) in *ver.* 41 Ephraim with *S* has ܓܒܪܐ ܚܕ 'a man, a money-lender,' while *C* and the Peshitta have ܚܕ ܡܢ ܪܒܘ 'a certain creditor.' That the reading of *S* and Ephraim was also that of the Diatessaron is clear from Moesinger, where however what appears in the Latin (p. 114) as *uni domino creditori* should be translated *viro cuidam feneratori* (ܡܢ ܚܕ ܪܒܘ). (2) In the beginning of *ver.* 43 both *S* and *C* have with Ephraim 'Simon saith to him,' while the Peshitta has more in accordance with the Greek 'Simon answered and said.' The simplification of these introductory sentences in dialogue is one of the characteristics of the Old Syriac, while the Peshitta tends to follow the Greek wording. It is therefore noteworthy that Ephraim here agrees with *S C* and not with the Peshitta. (3) At the end of *ver.* 43 Ephraim has ܬܪܝܨܐܝܬ 'correctly' in agreement with the Peshitta, while *S C* have ܫܦܝܪ 'well.' The word in the Greek is ὀρθῶς, which is translated by ܬܪܝܨܐܝܬ in Lk x 28, xx 21, by *S* and *C* as well as Pesh. In this passage the agreement of *S* and *C* shews us that ܫܦܝܪ was really the reading of the *Evangelion da-Mepharreshe*, which is therefore not the text from which Ephraim is quoting.[1]

Luke ix 62 = *Overbeck* 127

ܠܐ ܐܢܫ ܪܡܐ ܐܝܕܗ ܥܠ ܣܟܬܐ ܕܦܕܢܐ ܘܗܦܟ
ܠܒܣܬܪܗ: ܘܗܘܐ ܚܫܚ ܠܡܠܟܘܬܐ ܕܫܡܝܐ.

No one putteth his hand on the plough-share and looketh behind him, and becometh fit for the kingdom of heaven.

Here again Ephraim does not exactly reproduce any of the Syriac Biblical texts, for both *S C* and Pesh. have 'God,' not 'heaven.' But the insertion of ܗܘܐ 'becometh' is attested by *S C*.

---

[1] A parallel case is the rendering of ἐκδώσεται, which has been discussed above on Matt xxi 41.

Luke xii 49 = *Overbeck* 124, 126

ܢܘܪܐ ܐܬܝܬ ܕܐܪܡܐ ܒܐܪܥܐ.

Fire I came to cast in the earth.

This agrees with Pesh. against *S C*, which add ܗܘ ܓܝܪ after ܢܘܪܐ (*For fire it is that I came to cast...*).

Luke xii 54—56, [Matt] xvi 2, 3 = *Rom.* v 320 B

[56]ܦܪܨܘܦܐ ܠܡ ܓܝܪ ܕܐܪܥܐ. ܐܦ ܕܫܡܝܐ ܝܕܥܝܢ
ܐܢܬܘܢ [55]ܘܐܡܬܝ ܗܘܐ ܫܪܒܐ. [54]ܘܐܡܬܝ ܗܘܐ
ܡܛܪܐ. [Mt]ܡܬܢܒܝܢ ܐܦ ܥܠ ܨܚܘܐ. ܘ.[1]

For the face of the earth and of the heaven too ye know, and when there will be a sirocco and when there will be rain; prophecies are made also about fine weather.

This stanza is not a quotation, but is as Mr Woods calls it (p. 122) a 'mixed paraphrase' of Matt xvi 2, 3, and Luke xii 54—56. As a matter of fact it is only the last clause that seems to be taken from Matt., but the word ܨܚܘܐ 'fine weather' is decisive. S. Ephraim's Gospel text therefore included the interpolated verses, which are read in the Peshitta, but not in *S* or *C*. This quotation, therefore, is not taken from the *Evangelion da-Mepharreshe*. But neither is it from the Peshitta, for the word used corresponding to καύσων (Lk xii 55) is not ܚܘܡܐ 'heat,' as in the Peshitta, but ܫܪܒܐ 'a sirocco.' This is a somewhat rare word, ultimately derived from an Assyrian name for an oven. But it is used in this place by *C* and by *S* also.[2]

Ephraim's quotation here, therefore, presents similar features to those which we have noticed elsewhere; *viz.* it has the language and style of the *Evangelion da-Mepharreshe* or Old Syriac, but an independent text: in other words, it has the characteristic features of the

[1] I give the text from B.M. Add. 14571, *fol.* 33 v *a*. The Roman Edition has ܝܕܥܝܢ ܐܢܬܘܢ before ܐܦ ܕܫܡܝܐ, and inserts ܬܘܒ before ܡܛܪܐ to the ruin of the metre.

[2] The reading of *S* given in Mrs Lewis's *Some Pages* is ܕܚܘܡܐ, but Mrs Lewis's transcript had ܕܫܪܒܐ and the edited reading is merely the result of misapprehension.

Syriac Diatessaron. From this passage we further gain the very interesting information that the Diatessaron, like every other text known to be connected with the West, recognised the interpolation ὀψίας γενομένης κ.τ.λ. in Matt xvi 2, 3, which is absent from the best Greek texts (אB and Origen) as well as from the Old Syriac codices *C* and *S*.

Luke xiv 31 = *Rom.* v 487 A

ܟܬܝܒ ܕܐܝܢܐ ܗܘ ܡܢ ܡ̈ܠܟܐ. ܘܐܙܘܐ ܐܙܠ ܠܡܩܪܒ.
ܠܗ. ܥܡ ܡܠܟܐ ܐܚܪܢܐ ܚܒܪܗ.

It is written 'Who among kings goeth to do battle with another king his fellow?'

This is quite different both from Pesh. and from *S C*, and we really possess no evidence to shew whether Ephraim's wording is anything more than a paraphrase arranged to suit his 7-syllable metre.[1] But as the quotation is expressly introduced for the sake of the word ܚܒܪܗ which means his 'fellow' or 'comrade' (though in this case used of an enemy), it is evident that the word must have stood in Ephraim's text. In Lk xiv 31 *S C* both have ܡܠܟܐ ܐܚܪܢܐ, while the Peshitta has ܡܠܟܐ ܚܒܪܗ.

Luke xv 4 f.; see on Matt xviii 12 f.

Luke xvii 31, 32 = *Overbeck* 127

ܐܢ ܐܢܫ ܠܗ ܐܝܬܘܗܝ، ܒܫܘܩܐ ܘܡ̈ܐܢܘܗܝ، ܒܒܝܬܐ܇
ܠܐ ܢܥܘܠ ܘܢܣܒ ܐܢܘܢ܆ ܕܟܪܘ ܠܗ ܠܐܢܬܬܗ ܕܠܘܛ.

'If any one is in the street and his things in the house, let him not enter and take them. Recollect the wife of Lot.'

Here again the wording is different both from Pesh. and from *S C*, and the text of the Diatessaron is not given for this passage in

[1] A ܗܘ seems to have dropped out after ܟܬܝܒ. Some such word must be supplied for metrical reasons.

Moesinger. But the quotation from Ephraim is taken from a prose work, so that it may not be a simple paraphrase. The chief differences are that Ephraim has ܒܫܘܩܐ 'in the street' for ἐπὶ τοῦ δώματος, where the Syriac Biblical texts have ܒܐܓܪܐ 'in the roof' (Pesh.) or ܥܠ ܐܓܪܐ 'on the roof' (*S C*); and that Ephraim has ܐܬܕܟܪ 'recollect,' where the Syriac Biblical texts have ܐܬܕܟܪܘ 'remember.' The omissions made by Ephraim at the end of xvii 31 are probably of no importance, as he speaks of 'our Lord telling us not to turn back' (*cf ver*. 31[b]), just before his more formal quotation begins.

Luke xviii 13 = *Overbeck* 28

ܡܛܠ ܕܚܠܬܗ ܡܢܝܚ ܐܙܠܐ ܕܢܪܝܡ ܥܝܢܘܗܝ ܠܐ ܡܡܪܚ ܗܘܐ.

He [*the publican*] *because of his fear was not daring to lift his eyes to heaven.*

The Greek has οὐκ ἤθελεν...ἐπᾶραι, and accordingly *S* and the Peshitta have *he was not willing to lift*. But *C* agrees with Ephraim, against the Greek.

It is an obvious step to go on and assume that 'was not daring' is the reading of the lost Diatessaron, and this conjecture is borne out by the interesting fact that the reading comes to the surface again in Latin, not in one of the leading representatives of the Old Latin, but in the well-known Codex Sangermanensis *g*, Wordsworth's G. One of the constituent elements of this mixed and curious text seems to have been an early Latin text of the Diatessaron,[1] and doubtless it was from the Diatessaron that it came to read here *nec oculos ad caelum leuare audebat*.

Luke xxii 43, 44 = *Lamy* i 233, 655, *Nis.* 59[229]

The passages from *Lamy* i 665 and *Nis*. 59 only shew in a general way that S. Ephraim's Gospel text contained the incident of the bloody sweat. In this it agrees with *C*, the Peshitta, and *Moes*. 235, but

---

[1] See especially Lk xxiii 48.

differs from S. The passage from *Lamy* i 233 goes more into detail and is worth quoting :

ܘܚܙܐ ܕܡܠܐܟܐ ܠܗ ܕܐܬܚܙܝ ܟܬܝܒ ܗܘ.

It is written that there appeared to him an angel strengthening him.

Here C and Ephraim agree in omitting 'from heaven' after 'angel,' against the Peshitta and all other authorities, except a few patristic quotations (including Arius and Caesarius of Nazianzus). Wherever therefore C and Ephraim got their common text of this passage, it was not from the Peshitta.

Luke xxiii 38 = *Lamy* i 667

ܛܘܒܝܟܝ ܦܬܠܐ.

Happy art thou, O tablet!

The same word ܦܬܠܐ, a Syriac adaptation of πιττακιον, is used also in S and C for the ἐπιγραφή of the Gospel text. But the Peshitta has ܟܬܒܐ, which must have been regarded as a more literal translation, as it is here found also in the Harclean.

Luke xxiii 43 = *Lamy* i 667, 669

(667) ܣܓܕ ܠܓܠܓܘܬܐ ܦܬܚ ܘܥܠ.

From thee [Golgotha] he opened and entered Eden.

(669) ܡܪܢ ܕܒܪ ܘܣܡܟܝ ܒܥܕܢ.

Our Lord took and set thee [the thief] in Eden.

It is evident from these passages that Ephraim read 'in the garden of Eden' with C, Aphraates, and the Diatessaron (*Moes.* 244, 245), not 'in Paradise' with S and the Peshitta.

The quotations of S. Ephraim from the beginning of the Fourth Gospel present several peculiarities and difficulties, and it is probable that he had not always the same text before him. The full bearing of his quotations can hardly be appreciated without giving long extracts.

Joh i 1 = *Lamy* ii 513

In the beginning He was the Word.

This agrees verbally both with *C* and Pesh., but the English translation here given (which is demanded by the context) assumes ܡܠܬܐ 'word' to be feminine as in *C*, not masculine as in Pesh. *S* is deficient until Joh i 25.

Joh i 3 = *Rom.* iv 18 E

The Evangelist saith of him '*Every thing was in Him, and apart from Him not even one thing was.*'

This exactly agrees with the *Evangelion da-Mepharreshe* as represented by *C*, but the Peshitta has ܟܠ ܒܐܝܕܗ ܗܘܐ, i.e. 'all was through Him' (following the Greek πάντα δι' αὐτοῦ ἐγένετο), instead of ܟܠ ܒܗ ܗܘܐ. The rendering of *C* and Ephraim is also found in the Syriac *Theophania* i 24.

Joh i 3 = *Lamy* ii 513 f. (corrected from B.M. Add. 12164)

From the same [*S. Ephraim*]. *For John started to write that which our Lord endured in Himself.* "*Now he began with the history of the Son from where* (*it says*) *that* '*Through Him had been created everything*'......*John therefore left* (*the consideration of*) *that which through Him had been created*..."

These words, as may be seen from the opening formula, are taken from a collection of extracts. The collection is that made by Philoxenus at the end of his great and still unedited work on the Incarnation, written to prove 'that One Person of the Trinity became Man,' which is preserved in a Vatican MS and also in B.M. Add. 12164, a MS of the 6th century. It is perfectly clear that the version of Joh i 3 agrees with the Peshitta, and differs from *C* and Ephraim's quotation elsewhere, in having ܒܐܝܕܗ for δι' αὐτοῦ. At the same time, it differs both from *C* and the Peshitta in having ܐܬܒܪܝܘ 'created,' instead of ܗܘܐ 'was,' to render ἐγένετο. This is not unparalleled in Syriac texts of the Gospel; in Mk ii 27 ܐܬܒܪܝ seems to stand for ἐγένετο in *S* and the Peshitta, but curiously enough not in the Diatessaron (*Moes.* 62); nor is there any thing in the opening section of Ephraim's Commentary on the Diatessaron (*Moes.* 6) to suggest that it had ܐܬܒܪܝܘ in Joh i 3. Finally, Ephraim has ܟܠ ܡܕܡ in each place in agreement with *C*, where Pesh. has ܟܠ. The texts used by Ephraim in the beginning of the Fourth Gospel are thus diverse and their source is not at all clear, but none of them can be explained from the use of the Peshitta.

Joh i 14 = *Lamy* ii 743

ܡܠܬܗ ܕܐܒܐ ܐܬܬ ܡܢ ܥܘܒܗ. ܘܠܒܫܬ ܦܓܪܐ.
ܒܥܘܒܐ ܐܚܪܢܐ. ܡܢ ܥܘܒܐ ܠܥܘܒܐ ܢܦܩܬ. ܘܡܠܘ
ܡܢܗ ܥܘܒܐ ܢܟܦܐ. ܒܪܝܟ ܕܫܪܐ ܒܢ.

The Word of the Father came from His bosom, and clothed itself with a body in another bosom; from bosom to bosom it went forth, and pure bosoms have been filled from it: blessed is He that dwelleth in us!

It is obvious that this is a reference to Joh i 14 and 18, the reference to 'bosoms' shewing that the Biblical statement is in the mind of the writer and not a generalised reference to the Incarnation. But the diction in two very important particulars is that of *C* and not of the Peshitta; the Word is feminine, and It puts on not flesh (ܒܣܪܐ), but a body (ܦܓܪܐ). For ὁ λόγος σὰρξ ἐγένετο Pesh. has ܡܠܬܐ ܒܣܪܐ ܗܘܐ, but *C* has ܡܠܬܐ ܦܓܪܐ ܗܘܬ, and Aphraates twice quotes the verse in agreement with *C*. That the Peshitta gives the revision and *C* the original Syriac rendering is made highly probable by the fact that even the Peshitta has ܦܓܪܐ in all seven places where σὰρξ occurs in the sixth chapter of S. John. It is not necessary here to examine the reasons which led to the original adoption of the term 'body' in Joh i 13, 14, or to those which led to the subsequent rejection of it in favour of a more literal rendering of the Greek.[1] But I may remark that there is no surer test of the Biblical text used by a Syriac author than the phrase used for the Incarnation. On the one hand the Acts of Thomas, the Doctrine of Addai, Aphraates and S. Ephraim, constantly speak of our Lord having 'clothed Himself with a body'; on the other, Isaac of Antioch and the biographer of Rabbula agree with the Peshitta in speaking of the Word made *flesh*, a phrase which (so far as I know) never occurs in Syriac literature before the 5th century.

This passage also is quoted by Philoxenus (B.M. Add. 12164, *fol.* 131 r *a*), with the reading ܘܗܘܬ ܦܓܪܐ '*and became a body.*' This reading is exactly what is found in *C*, and as it is metrically satisfactory it may very well be the actual wording used by S. Ephraim.

John iii 34 = *Lamy* i 267

ܡܛܠ ܗܢܐ ܠܐ ܗܘܐ ܒܡܫܘܚܬܐ ܝܗܒ ܠܗ ܐܒܘܗܝ ܪܘܚܐ.

Therefore not by measure gave his Father to him the Spirit.

This passage presents several interesting variants in Syriac texts, which can best be exhibited by quotation in full. We have

ܠܐ ܗܘܐ ܒܡܫܘܚܬܐ ܝܗܒ ܠܗ ܐܒܘܗܝ ܪܘܚܐ *Ephr Aph* 122

„ „ „ ܝܗܒ ܪܘܚܐ ܐܒܐ ܠܒܪܗ *Aph* 123

[1] See Isho'dad as quoted by Dr J. R. Harris in *Fragments of the Commentary of Ephrem Syrus upon the Diatessaron*, p. 25. The Armenian altogether fails us here, for in Armenian Մարմին *marmin* stands indifferently for σὰρξ and for σῶμα.

ܠܐ ܗܘܐ ܓܝܪ ܒܟܝܠܬܐ ܝܗܒ . . ܐܒܐ ܠܒܪܗ *C* (partly torn away)
ܠܐ ܗܘܐ ܓܝܪ ܒܟܝܠܬܐ ܝܗܒ ܐܠܗܐ ܐܒܐ *S*vid
ܒܟܝܠܐ ܝܗܒ ܐܠܗܐ ܪܘܚܐ ,, ,, ,, Pesh.

As to *S*, ܐܠܗܐ is not legible in the photograph. *Moes.* 105 has 'And not by measure gave he to his Son.'

The Greek of this passage is οὐ γὰρ ἐκ μέτρου δίδωσιν [ὁ θεὸς] τὸ πνεῦμα, followed by ὁ πατὴρ ἀγαπᾷ τὸν υἱόν. If ܐܠܗܐ be really the reading of *S*, it looks almost like a conflation with syr.vg; but the independence of Ephraim in this passage needs no further comment.[1]

Joh vi 52 = *Rom.* vi 102 F

ܐܝܟܢ ܡܨܐ ܗܢܐ ܦܓܪܗ ܢܬܠ ܠܢ.

How can this man his body give us?

This is a mere allusion, with ܠܡܐܟܠ 'to eat' at the end of the verse left out and ܐܝܟܢ ܡܨܐ (3 syllables) substituted for the Biblical ܐܝܟܢܐ ܡܫܟܚ (5 syllables), doubtless for metrical reasons. At the same time it agrees in giving the order found in Pesh. against ܢܬܠ ܠܢ ܦܓܪܗ in *S C*. The order here preserved in Pesh. and Ephraim is that of cod. 69, and partially that of other MSS of the 'Ferrar Group.'

Joh xii 2 (Luke x 40) = *Lamy* i 255

ܟܕ ܡܪܬܐ ܥܢܝܐ ܗܘܬ ܒܬܫܡܫܬܐ

When Martha was occupied in serving...

This sentence belongs properly to Lk x 40 (ἡ δὲ Μάρθα περιεσπᾶτο περὶ πολλὴν διακονίαν), but it appears in Ephraim as part of the story of the supper given by Lazarus and his sisters to Christ. Thus it corresponds to Joh xii 2 (καὶ ἡ Μάρθα διηκόνει), a clause which is literally translated in the Peshitta. But *S* actually has in Joh xii 2 ܡܪܬܐ ܕܝܢ ܥܢܝܐ ܗܘܬ ܒܬܫܡܫܬܐ.

[1] Note that ܟܝܠܐ is peculiar to syr.vg, as it has now been definitely ascertained that *S* reads ܒܟܝܠܬܐ (*Expositor* for Aug., 1897, p. 117).

What makes the agreement here of *S* and Ephraim all the more remarkable is that the Diatessaron, as represented in *Moes.* 99, 204, and also in the Arabic, kept the two incidents quite distinct. But in Ephraim they are completely confused.

Joh xiii 5 = *Lamy* i 657

[Syriac text]

Our Lord purified the bodily frame of the brethren, in a dish which is the symbol of concord.

For εἰς τὸν νιπτῆρα in Joh xiii 5 the Peshitta has [Syriac] 'in a washing-bason,' but *S* and Aphraates have [Syriac] [Syriac] 'in a dish for washing.' This is evidently the text known to Ephraim.

The case is therefore exactly similar to Lk xxiii 38. There Ephraim and *S C* agreed in having [Syriac], a word derived from πιττάκιον, but used as a translation of ἐπιγραφή. Here Ephraim agrees with Aphraates and *S* in having [[Syriac]] [Syriac], where [Syriac] is derived from λεκάνη, but is used to translate νιπτήρ.

Joh xiv 23 = *Lamy* i 273

[Syriac text]

'*He that loveth me, unto him we come, and an abode with him we will make.*'

The latter part of this verse is quoted also in Aphraates 130. The one MS of Aphraates (Wright's A) agrees with Ephraim and with *S* in having [Syriac] 'we will make.' The other MS of Aphraates (Wright's B) has [Syriac] 'we make' with the Peshitta.[1] *C*, on the other hand, has [Syriac] [Syriac] 'I come' and [Syriac] 'I will make,' in agreement with Codex Bezae and the Old Latin MS *e*. I have but little doubt that the true reading of the *Evangelion da-Mepharreshe* is given in *C*, and the reading of the Diatessaron is given in *S*, in Aphraates and in Ephraim.

[1] This is not the only occasion where cod. A of Aphraates gives a better reading than that of B or *B*.

Joh xv 1 = *Lamy* ii 359

ܟܪܡܐ ܕܩܘܫܬܐ
The Vineyard of Truth.

A number of indications combine to shew that this is a reference to Joh xv 1; or rather, that this is a reference to the passage in the Diatessaron corresponding to Joh xv 1, and that the Diatessaron had *I am the true Vineyard....and ye are the vines.*

The context of the passage quoted is not in itself quite decisive. S. Ephraim says of the loss of Nisibis to the heathen Persians : "The vineyard that belonged to my Beloved in a corner of fertile land (Isaiah v 1, *sic*), that vineyard hath the oppressor rooted up, and planted a new one in its stead. The vineyards of time are worked more than the Vineyard of Truth : wrath hath made all vineyards desolate, that in the Vineyard of verity we may work." No doubt Ephraim has also in mind the Parable of the Vineyard (Matt xx), but the phrase in S. John is the only one which connects either Vine or Vineyard with "truth."[1]

The verse is quoted again in a tract of S. Ephraim extant only in Armenian (Ephr. *Arm.* ii 292). After quoting Matt xxi 33, he goes on : "And again in another place He says *I am the Vineyard, and ye are the vine.*"[2]

Besides these passages from Ephraim we find other instances of the same rendering in early Syriac literature.

Aphraates says with unmistakeable reference to Joh xv 1 (*Wright*, p. 288) :

ܗܘܝܘ ܟܪܡܐ ܕܩܘܫܬܐ ܘܐܒܘܗܝ ܦܠܚܐ ܘܚܢܢ ܫܒܫܬܐ ܕܢܨܝܒܢ ܒܓܘܗ.

He is the Vineyard of Truth, and His Father the husbandman, and we the vines planted within Him.

And Cyrillona, at the end of the 4th century, says (*ZDMG* xxvii 580) :

ܣܒ ܠܟ ܒܗܠܐ ܕܐܠܗܐ. ܡܢܐ ܐܡܪ. ܟܪܡܐ ܐܢܐ ܐܢܐ. ܟܪܡܐ ܕܩܘܫܬܐ. ܘܐܒܐ ܗܘ ܐܟܪܘܡܐ ܕܝܠܗ.

---

[1] "Vine *of Truth*" is of course only the Semitic turn of expression for "*True Vine.*"

[2] The word translated 'Vineyard' is *այգի* (as in Matt xxi 33 arm.vg), that translated 'Vine' is *որթ* (as in Joh xv 1 arm.vg).

Let us see again how our Saviour hath used of Himself the similitude of a vineyard: 'I am the Vineyard of Truth, and my Father—He is the husbandman.'

But this curious mistranslation is not found in S or the Peshitta, though otherwise the two texts differ considerably in the opening words of Joh xv, nor is there any trace of it in the Acts of Thomas.[1] It is therefore probable that it never found its way into Biblical texts, though it seems to have been a characteristic feature of the Syriac Diatessaron.

Joh xvi 11 = *Rom.* iv 37 F

ܘܐܡܪ ܕܥܠ ܕܝܢܗ ܕܐܪܟܘܢܐ ܕܥܠܡܐ ܗܢܐ ܡܬܬܕܝܢ.

And he said 'About his judgement, that the ruler of this world is judged.'

Here S agrees with Ephraim in having ܕܐܪܟܘܢܐ, where Pesh. has ܐܪܟܘܢܐ, but both S and Pesh. have ܕܝܢܐ 'judgement' not ܕܝܢܗ 'his judgement.' How likely an early Syriac text was to have the suffix here is shewn by Joh xvi 8, where S has 'He will reprove the world in its sins and about his righteousness,' against the Greek and the Peshitta.

Joh xvii 11 = *Rom.* vi 122 c

ܐܒܝ ܣܒ ܘܛܪ ܐܢܘܢ

My Father, take (and) keep them.

B.M. Add. 12176 reads ܘܛܪ 'and keep.' Pesh. has ܐܒܐ ܩܕܝܫܐ ܛܪ ܐܢܘܢ 'Holy Father, keep them,' while S has ܐܒܝ ܩܕܝܫܐ ܣܒ ܘܛܪ ܐܢܘܢ 'My holy Father, take (and) keep them.' ܩܕܝܫܐ had of course to be dropped in making a 5-syllable verse, and its omission leaves just five syllables both in S and in Pesh. It is therefore significant that Ephraim should give the reading of S and not of the Peshitta.

---

[1] The words 'I have planted Thy vine in the land' (*Wright* 314[14] E. Tr. 280[15]) may refer rather to Matt xxi 33 : the vine is here the Gospel, rather than Christ or individual Christians.

Joh xix 30 = *Lamy* i 229

ܐܠܗܐ ܕܐܡܪ ܐܝܟ ܕܡܫܠܡ ܗܘܐ ܟܠܡܕܡ ܠܗ.

As he said 'Lo, every thing is finished.'

Neither *S* nor *C* is here extant, nor is the verse quoted in Moesinger, but the Arabic Diatessaron (lii 4) and the Armenian vulgate have 'Everything has been finished.' The Peshitta has only ܗܐ ܡܫܠܡ, so that here again Ephraim appears to be following the Diatessaron.

Joh xx 24 = *Rom.* vi 16 F

ܘܝܗܘܕܐ ܬܐܘܡܐ

And Judas Thomas.

This is the reading of the Vatican MS on which the Roman Edition professes to be based, as given in *Bibliotheca Orientalis* I 101, and it is also the reading of B.M. Add. 12176; the printed text changes it into ܬܐܘܡܐ ܘܠܗ, whereby both the metre is spoilt and the connexion with Old Syriac nomenclature is lost. Judas, or Judas Thomas, is the regular name for the apostle in the *Acta Thomae*, and the 'Judas not Iscariot' of John xiv 22 appears as '*Judas Thomas*' in *C* and '*Thomas*' in *S*. The name Judas Thomas also occurs in the Syriac Doctrine of Addai, and it was doubtless from a Syriac source that Eusebius got the Ἰούδας ὁ καὶ Θωμᾶς of *HE* i 13.

On the 48 passages quoted and discussed in the preceding pages must rest the decision as to what text of the Gospel was used by S. Ephraim. For my own part, I cannot think that the occasional coincidences of language with the Peshitta against the Sinai Palimpsest and the Curetonian, amounting to eight in all, are of a character to suggest the actual use of the Syriac Vulgate.[1] Most of them occur in passages which otherwise present notable coincidences with the Sinai Palimpsest or the Curetonian, or else differ widely from all known Syriac texts of the Gospel.

[1] The coincidences referred to are Matt xvi 2 (ܚܘܐ), Matt xxi 41 (ܐܘܒܕ), Mk xii 42 (ܫܡܢܝܢ), Lk vii 43 (ܕܝܬܝܪ ܚܒ), Lk xii 49 (*om.* ܥܠ ܗܘ), Lk xiv 31 (ܠܘܚܡܐ), Joh i 3 (ܐܬܒܪܝ) and Joh vi 52 (*order*).

Against these are to be set at least three times as many agreements of S. Ephraim with *S* or *C* against the Peshitta, some of them of most striking and unmistakeable character. The phrases 'My Son and My beloved' at the Baptism, 'the sons' table' in the story of the Syro-Phoenician woman, the statements that Hanna the prophetess had lived only seven *days* with her husband and that the publican in the Temple did not *dare* to lift up his eyes to heaven, the words used for the *tablet* on the Cross and for the *dish* which Christ used to wash the disciples' feet, the promise of *Eden* to the penitent thief, the name of *Judas* Thomas, and last but by no means least the statement that the Word became *a body*—all these S. Ephraim shares with 'Old Syriac' MSS, and with Old Syriac MSS or the Diatessaron alone.

There are not wanting also marked differences between S. Ephraim and these MSS, and these differences suggest that it was not the Old Syriac version of the Four Gospels, the *Evangelion da-Mepharreshe*, that S. Ephraim was using, but the Diatessaron. Whatever the origin of the Syriac Diatessaron may have been, and I see no reason to doubt the correctness of the tradition that it was the Harmony made by Tatian the disciple of Justin Martyr, it is certain that in S. Ephraim's day the wording of the text was very largely the wording of the *Evangelion da-Mepharreshe*. The agreements of S. Ephraim with *S* and *C* are all explicable on the supposition that he was using the Diatessaron, while in many of the differences the reading attested by S. Ephraim is known on other grounds to have been that of the Diatessaron. This is the case with the curious statements that our Lord spat on His fingers when healing the deaf man, that He was actually thrown down from the cliff by the people of Nazareth, and that He said at the end 'Lo, everything is finished.' S. Ephraim also agrees with the express testimony of Aphraates, who seems to have used the Diatessaron habitually if not exclusively, that Christ said to the widow's son 'Youth, youth, arise!'—a form of the saying otherwise only found in the West.

I do not shrink from going yet further, and using the testimony of S. Ephraim to establish the presence in the Diatessaron of the saying about the Face of the Sky and the episode of the Bloody Sweat, neither of which belong to the true text of the Old Syriac version of the Four Gospels, though found in the Peshitta. The latter of these passages is quoted in the Commentary on the Diatessaron and has found its way into the Curetonian MS, but the former one does not happen to be mentioned in the Commentary and it is omitted in the Curetonian MS as well as in the Sinai Palimpsest. Thus it is only by the chance quotation of S. Ephraim that it is attested for any ancient Syriac text. At the same time in each of these two important passages the text as quoted by S. Ephraim has marked divergences from the Peshitta, so that the presence of these quotations in S. Ephraim cannot be used to prove his use of that version.

Rabbula's revision of the Syriac N.T.

The quotations of S. Ephraim from the Gospel, therefore, afford no proof of the use of the Peshitta, the Syriac Vulgate. As far as S. Ephraim is concerned, that familiar text, found with so little variation in so many ancient codices, may not yet have been in existence. We are free to bring down the date of its appearance to a later period, to the 5th century. It only remains to point out a passage in Syriac literature which now may be plausibly conjectured to tell the story of its first publication. If I am right, the great event took place soon after 411 AD under the auspices of Rabbula, who had been in that year appointed bishop of Edessa.

Rabbula's first care, after making some necessary regulations for the better ordering of Divine Service, was for a more accurate version of the New Testament. "He translated," says his biographer, "by the wisdom of God that was in him the New Testament from Greek into Syriac, because of its variations, exactly as it was" (*Overbeck* 172, quoted also in Wright's *Syriac Literature*, p. 11). It is only the belief, the erroneous belief, that the Peshitta N.T. was proved to be older than Rabbula through the attestation given to it by S. Ephraim, which has hitherto prevented scholars from recognising in these words a description of the making and publication of the Syriac Vulgate. "La version de Rabboula ne peut être...la Peschitto que saint Ephrem connaissait déjà" says, for instance, M. Rubens Duval in his admirable *Littérature Syriaque*, p. 48, but when S. Ephraim's acquaintance with the Peshitta is denied the argument falls to the ground. And the identification of the Peshitta N.T. with Rabbula's revision satisfies yet another condition of the problem. We are often told that if the Peshitta be the result of a revision it must have left a trace in history: here, then, is the actual record of the revision, just in the historical setting that suits it best.

The authority of Rabbula secured an instant success for the new revised version. The whole tendency of the age was towards closer union with Greek thought and Greek theology, and the Diatessaron from that moment was doomed. It was during Rabbula's episcopate and through his efforts that the remnant of the Bardesanians joined the Catholic Church (*Overbeck* 192), whereby the only body which might have clung to the unrevised Syriac texts of the Gospels was wiped out. Copies of the Peshitta were rapidly multiplied; it soon became the only text in ecclesiastical use, and it is quoted by all succeeding ecclesiastical writers. The only rival it had in later times to face was the Monophysite revision by Thomas of Harkel, a still more literal rendering of the Greek text.

APPENDIX I.

S. Ephraim's Quotations from the Prologue to the Fourth Gospel.

The questions raised by S. Ephraim's quotations from the opening verses of the Gospel according to S. John group themselves naturally under three heads. These are: (1) What evidence is there that he knew the Fourth Gospel as a separate work, apart from the *Diatessaron*? (2) Is there any reason to suppose that he used two independent texts of Joh i 3? (3) What was the exact meaning of his text of the opening words?

(1) With regard to the first head the evidence is as follows. Philoxenus of Mabbog collected at the end of his treatise on the Trinity a number of passages from earlier writers in support of his own views. This collection is extant in B.M. Add. 12164, itself a MS of the 6th century, and includes some passages from the lost homily of S. Ephraim on Joh i 1. These have been edited in *Lamy* ii 513 f.: it would have been an advantage if all the Ephraim extracts had been printed, so that we might have some idea of the standard of correctness aimed at by Philoxenus I give the extract in full, as it is also interesting with regard to the question of Ephraim's text of Joh i 3.

Lamy ii 513 f. (corrected from B.M. Add. 12164)

[Syriac text]

"*Again, from the same* [S. Ephraim], *out of the Discourse upon* '*In the beginning was the Word.*' Now what is 'The same that was in the beginning,' but 'The same that, lo, to-day by means of His advent hath been known, Who hath been declared to be God'?

"*From the same.* For John started to write that which our Lord suffered in His own person. Now he began with the story of the Son from where (it says) 'Through Him was created everything,' that he might tell in one sentence concerning those things that were through Him and concerning those things that were in His own person; so that because of the great things that were through Him we might know to what lowliness He had descended, to whose person the shameful deeds were done.

"By John therefore saying 'In the beginning,' he hath in fact called Moses to witness, that Moses might give witness concerning those things that were through the Son, that he might induce us accurately to investigate those things that were done to His person. Of old, therefore, through Him were all good things made for the universe, and at the last were all evil things made by mankind: John therefore left that which through Him had been created and began to

---

[1] [Syriac] Cod. 12164 (*sic*).

tell concerning that which He suffered in His own person. For when the witness began that through Him were wonderful things created, he started to tell that to His person the shameful deeds were done."

Similar testimony is borne by one of S. Ephraim's *Hymns De Fide* (Ed. Rom. vi 62):—

ܕܪܺܝܫܳܐ ܫܰܪܺܝ ܫܰܪܺܝ . ܘܳܐܦ ܝܽܘܚܰܢܳܢ ܐܰܟ ܡܽܘܫܶܐ ܐܳܘ ܒܪܺܝܫܳܐ ܕܟܬܳܒܝܗܘܢ . ܚܰܟܺܝܡܳܐܺܝܬ ܕܪܰܫܳܥܺܝ ܠܟܳܬܒܶܐ ܫܰܪܺܝ

The one 'In the beginning' is like the other 'In the beginning,' and like unto Moses is John also, in that at the beginning of their writings they confuted the writers that cavilled wickedly.

It is difficult to resist the conclusion that S. Ephraim was aware that the passage which stood at the head of the *Diatessaron* was the beginning of S. John's Gospel. But these two references stand alone: I do not think that any other allusion to the individual Evangelists is to be found in his genuine works.

(2) The text of Joh i 3, as quoted in the above extract, presents some difficulty. The natural inference would be that the clause corresponding to πάντα δι' αὐτοῦ ἐγένετο was in Syriac

ܒܐܺܝܕܶܗ ܐܶܬܒܪܺܝ ܟܽܠ ܡܶܕܶܡ

Through Him was created every thing.

But this is the reading neither of the Peshitta, nor of the *Evangelion da-Mepharreshe*, nor of Ephraim himself elsewhere. The Peshitta has

ܟܽܠ ܒܐܺܝܕܶܗ ܗܘܳܐ

All through Him was.

The *Evangelion da-Mepharreshe*, on the other hand, as represented by *C* (the leaf of *S* which contained the first twenty-four verses of S. John being unfortunately lost), has

ܟܽܠܡܶܕܶܡ ܒܶܗ ܗܘܳܐ

Everything in Him was,

and this rendering is supported by S. Ephraim's quotation of the passage in his Commentary on Genesis (Ed. Rom. iv 18 E).[1]

Of course it would be convenient if we could assume that S. Ephraim's quotation in the Commentary on Genesis was taken from the *Evangelion da-Mepharreshe*, and that his quotation in the Homily on John i 1 cited by Philoxenus was taken from the *Diatessaron*. Or again, it is possible that *Through Him was created everything* is the true text of the *Evangelion da-Mepharreshe*; and that the reading of *C*, like so many others in that MS, is a corruption from the *Diatessaron*: this, at least, would explain the pointed reference to 'John' in the extract cited by Philoxenus. It may be pointed out in this connexion that both *S* and the Peshitta have 'was created' in Mark ii 27, but the *Diatessaron* (*Moes*. 62) has the exact equivalent of ἐγένετο. There is, however, at this point a various reading ἐκτίσθη for ἐγένετο, which is not the case in S. John.

But whether S. Ephraim in this instance made use of two texts of Joh i 3 at different times, or whether the variations in the Philoxenus extract are only due to a confused recollection of Col i 16, it is at least noteworthy that none of S. Ephraim's quotations of this theologically important phrase agrees with the text of the Peshitta.

(3) There is very little doubt about the Syriac text of the first two verses of the Gospel according to S. John, which were also the first two verses of the *Diatessaron*. Both in the Peshitta and in *C* we read

ܒܪܫܝܬ ܐܝܬܘܗܝ ܗܘܐ ܡܠܬܐ . ܘܗܘ ܡܠܬܐ ܐܝܬܘܗܝ ܗܘܐ ܠܘܬ ܐܠܗܐ . ܘܐܠܗܐ ܐܝܬܘܗܝ ܗܘܐ ܗܘ ܡܠܬܐ . ܗܘܐ ܒܪܫܝܬ ܠܘܬ ܐܠܗܐ .

and this text is supported by quotations in Aphraates and S. Ephraim.

The difficulty lies in the circumstance that the verbs are masculine, while ܡܠܬܐ 'word' is feminine in Syriac; so that the Syriac for 'In the beginning was the Word and that word was with God' should be ܒܪܫܝܬ ܐܝܬܝܗ ܗܘܬ ܡܠܬܐ . ܘܗܝ ܡܠܬܐ ܐܝܬܝܗ ܗܘܬ ܠܘܬ ܐܠܗܐ . It is commonly said that ܡܠܬܐ (*mellĕthâ*) when it means

---

[1] See above, p. 48.

'God, the Word,' is treated as masculine, and this is true of later Syriac usage, beginning with the Peshitta itself. Thus in Joh i 14, for καὶ ὁ λόγος σὰρξ ἐγένετο καὶ ἐσκήνωσεν ἐν ἡμῖν, the Peshitta has

And the Word became flesh and sojourned with us.

But the corresponding words in C are

And the Word became a body and it sojourned with us,

and, as has been already pointed out on pp. 49, 50, this rendering is supported by Aphraates and by S. Ephraim (*Lamy* ii 743). If the Word be grammatically feminine in verse 14, it is not likely to have been treated as masculine in verse 1. Thus in the Old Syriac of Joh i 1 ܡܠܬܐ is feminine and so cannot be the subject of the masculine verb. We must therefore translate

In the beginning He was the Word; and He, the Word, was with God, and He, the Word, was God. The same was in the beginning with God.

With this translation the reason of the insertion of ܗܘ becomes clear. It is not a mere equivalent of the Greek article, but the actual nominative of the verbs, and ܡܠܬܐ is in apposition to it. Instead of being the subject of the Prologue, the fact that the Subject of the Prologue was the Word is the first statement made.

How far this is a legitimate treatment of the Greek is not for me to say, but the translation given above is the only one which is consistent with the treatment of 'The Word' as a feminine in Joh i 14, so that I believe it to be the true meaning of the Syriac. It also appears to me to be implied in the extracts given below from the same lost Homily of S. Ephraim on Joh i 1, which I reproduce from *Lamy* ii 511, as much from their intrinsic importance as for illustrations of the immediate point at issue. They are both preserved in a *Catena* of passages collected to prove that the ancient Fathers of the Church did not agree with Julian of Halicarnassus in thinking that our Lord's human Body was in its nature incorruptible.

Lamy ii 511 (corrected from B.M. Add. 14529)

ܟܕ ܣܠܩܘ ܡܟܝܠ ܡܢ ܡܨܪܝܢ. ܘܟܕ ܢܚܬܝܢ ܠܒܒܠ. ܒܫܘܪܝܐ
ܘܒܫܘܠܡܐ ܬܪ̈ܬܝܢ ܙܒ̈ܢܝܢ ܐܩܕܡܝܗܘܢ ܐܬܚܒܠܬ ܡܠܬܐ ܗܝ ܕܠܐ
ܡܬܚܒܠܢܐ. ܗܝ ܕܒܚܘܒܗܘܢ ܠܒܫܬ ܠܒܘܫܐ ܡܬܚܒܠܢܐ. ܗܢܘ ܕܝܢ
ܠܘ̈ܚܐ ܕܐܬܬܒܪܘ. ܘܡܓܠܬܐ ܕܐܬܦܣܩܬ. ܕܬܠܬ ܕܝܢ ܙܒ̈ܢܝܢ. ܚܠܦ ܗ̈ܠܝܢ
ܡ̈ܠܐ ܕܐܦ ܕܐܠܗܐ ܗ̈ܘܝ ܐܠܐ ܩ̈ܠܬ ܗ̈ܘܝ ܕܢܒܝܘܬܐ.
ܢܚܬ ܠܗ ܒܫܪܪܐ ܡܠܬܗ ܕܐܠܗܐ. ܗܘ ܕܠܐ ܗܘܐ ܡܠܬ ܒܪ ܐܢܫܐ
ܘܐܦܠܐ ܙܡܝܪܬܐ ܕܢܒܝܘܬܐ. ܘܐܦܠܐ ܩܠܬܐ ܕܫܠܝܚܘܬܐ. ܐܠܐ
ܡܠܬܐ. ܕܒܡ̈ܠܝܢ ܠܐ ܡܬܬܪܓܡܐ. ܘܒܦܘܡܢ ܠܐ ܡܬܡܠܠܐ ܘܒܠܫܢܢ
ܠܐ ܡܬܦܫܩܐ. ܘܒܙܡܝܪܢ ܠܐ ܡܬܚܣܢܐ. ܘܒܟܢܪܢ ܠܐ ܡܙܕܡܪܐ.
ܘܒܟܢܪܢ ܠܐ ܡܬܢܩܫܐ. ܘܒܐܬ̈ܘܬܢ ܠܐ ܡܬܡܟܟܐ. ܘܒܣܦܪܢ
ܠܐ ܡܬܟܬܒܐ. ܗܝ ܗܕܐ ܒܚܘܒܗ ܐܬܓܫܡܬ. ܘܠܒܫܬ ܦܓܪܐ
ܕܐܢܫܘܬܐ. ܕܬܬܠ ܚܝܐ ܠܐܢܫܘܬܐ. ܘܐܬܬ ܒܥܘܒܐ ܢܘܚ ܐܝܟ
ܕܒܥܘܒܐ ܐܪܥܐ. ܘܟܕ ܢܚܬ ܡܛܘܠ ܐܝܟ ܙ̈ܪܥܐ. ܘܦܪ̈ܝܐ
ܘܦܪ̈ܝܥܐ ܐܝܟ ܢܘ̈ܢܝܢ ܡܠܝܐ. ܦܪܚ ܘܣܠܩ ܠܘܬܗ ܐܝܟ ܕܒܪܘܝܐ.
ܘܡܪ̈ܓܐ ܕܦܫܚܐ ܢܚܬ ܠܡܥܡܩܗ ܒܝܬܐ. ܐܝܟ ܙ̈ܪܥܐ ܘܚܒ̈ܘܫܝ.
ܕܡܦܢܝܐ ܢܚܬ ܒܝܬܐ ܒܗ. ܕܒܗ ܐܝܟ ܕܒܡܥܡܩܐ ܥܒܪܐ ܗܘܬ
ܡܠܬ ܢܒܝܘܬܐ. ܗܝ ܕܐܬܝܬܗ ܕܒܘܬܗ ܘܫܘܠܡܗ ܕܡܠܬܐ ܚܕܬܐ
ܘܫܪܪܬܐ ܡܠܬܐ ܕܐܠܗܐ.

"When therefore they [i.e. Israel] came up from Egypt and when they were just going down to Babylon, at the beginning and at the end, on two occasions in their presence was destroyed the indestructible Word, which for love of them had clothed itself with clothing that could be destroyed, namely the Tables of Stone that were broken, and the Roll that was cut in pieces. But the third time, instead of these Words which, though they were God's, yet were only utterances of prophecy, there came down, being in truth the Word of God, He that was not a word of man nor a song of prophecy nor a voice of apostleship, but the Word which by our words cannot be interpreted, and by our mouth cannot be spoken and by our tongue cannot be explained, neither in our song contained nor with our lyre sung nor by our harp played nor with our letters spelt nor in our book written down—this very Word in its love condescended and clothed itself with a body of human nature that it might give life to human nature. And it came in the days of John as in the days of Jeremiah; and when Herod like Zedekiah saw it, and the scribes also like the king's nobles, they went mad and rebelled against it as if in wrath, and with the iron nails of the Cross they destroyed its outer clothing, like Zedekiah and his companions, who with an iron blade destroyed all the roll wherein as if embodied was dwelling the word of prophecy, which is the likeness and shadow of the only and true Word, the Word of God."

[Syriac text]

And after some other things (he goes on to say):

"Now from the beginning those creatures which had not existed were created through the Son. But at the last He clothed Himself with a Body that could be destroyed, that with the destruction of His Body the creatures that were destroyed might be renewed. It was right therefore that with a Word incapable of suffering the creatures without suffering should be created, and with a Body capable of destruction the creatures that were destroyed should be renewed. For these creatures without toil were being created from the beginning through the Son: therefore in the beginning He was the Word, a thing without toil, that by the meaning of His name thou mayest learn His true nature; but at the last with a Body which is destroyed He restored the creatures that were destroyed, that by the destruction of His true Body thou mayest learn the true destruction of the creatures."

APPENDIX II.

On some of the less well attested works of S. Ephraim.

For the purposes of this Essay it was needful not only to exclude from our consideration writings wrongly attributed to S. Ephraim, but also to base our conclusions upon those only of his writings in which the text was well preserved. To avoid any appearance of partiality in the selection I confined the list given on pp. 24, 25 of this book to those works of which we still possess at least one MS which goes back to the time before the great Mohammedan conquests in the 7th century. This arbitrary rule is, I believe, an infallible method for excluding spurious pieces, but it is certain to have excluded some genuine works also. I propose therefore in this Appendix to shew that some of the works ascribed to S. Ephraim which are now found only in later MSS contain Gospel quotations of a type similar to those in the better preserved works. Where this is the case we can be sure that the works in question are the genuine writings of S. Ephraim, while at the same time we glean a few more details about the Biblical text used by him.

The Testament of Ephraim.

This is perhaps the best known of all S. Ephraim's writings. It is the Saint's Last Will and Testament, of course not a legal document, but a metrical homily written in 7-syllable lines. Assemani, Wright, and now lately Dr Gwynn, all agree in accepting it as in the main genuine, though certainly interpolated. It is extant in several MSS,

SOME LESS WELL ATTESTED WORKS. 67

the oldest being B.M. Add. 14624, of the 7th or 8th cent. A shorter recension is preserved in B.M. Add. 14582 (dated AD 816), but this is said to be only an abridgement of the longer recension.

The *Testament* was edited from Cod. Vat. Syr. cxvii (12th cent.) by J. S. Assemani in vol. ii of the Roman Edition, as an appendix to the Greek translation of S. Ephraim: a better text is given in *Overbeck* 137—156.

The only Gospel allusion in the *Testament* of any textual interest is *Overbeck* 149[24] (*Rom.* ii 405 E) = Matt v 18

܀ܢܶܥܒܰܪ ܠܳܐ ܝܽܘܕ-ܐܳܬ݂ܳܐ ܘܚܰܕ ܂ ܢܶܥܒܪܽܘܢ ܘܐܰܪܥܳܐ ܫܡܰܝܳܐ

For heaven and earth pass away, and not a Jôd-letter will pass away.

The general turn of the sentence is taken from Matt xxiv 35, but 'one Jôd-letter' is the peculiar rendering of ἰῶτα ἓν ἢ μία κεραία found in Aphraates and in *S* at Matt v 18, while *C* has the double rendering 'one Jôd-letter or one horn.' But the Peshitta has ܝܘܕ ܐܘ ܚܕ ܢܘܢ ܣܪܛܐ 'one Jôd or one line,' an independent rendering which follows the wording of the Greek.

It is right to add that this passage of the *Testament* is absent from B.M. 14582.

The Hymns on the Epiphany.

These Hymns have been edited in the first volume of Lamy's *Ephraim* from MSS in the British Museum, the oldest of which (Add. 14506, *foll.* 166 ff.) is of the 9th or 10th century. The only allusion which throws light on the text is

Lamy i 127 = Matt iii 16

܀ܠܥܳܠܡܳܐ ܥܰܠ ܢܽܘܗܪܶܗ ܘܰܕܠܰܩ ܂ ܣܠܶܩ ܘܡܶܚܕܳܐ ܩܰܕܺܝܫܳܐ ܥܡܰܕ

The Holy one was baptised and immediately came up, and His light flamed upon the world.

Neither the Peshitta nor the *Evangelion da-Mepharreshe* have any allusion to the Light at our Lord's Baptism, but it clearly had a place

5—2

in the Diatessaron. Not only does Ephraim himself speak of 'the shining of the light which was on the waters' (*Moes.* 43), but the Syriac text of the Diatessaron itself was quoted by the common source of Isho'dad and Barsalibi for the sake of the addition. Barsalibi is still unedited, but the quotation from Isho'dad is given by Dr Harris in his *Fragments of the Commentary of Ephrem Syrus upon the Diatessaron.*

The passage from Barsalibi's Commentary on the Gospels runs as follows (B.M. Add. 7184, *fol.* 37)

[Syriac text]

And immediately, as the Gospel of the Diatessaron (i.e. the Mixed) testifies, a mighty light flashed upon the Jordan and the river was girdled with white clouds, and there appeared his many hosts that were uttering praise in the air; and Jordan stood still from its flowing, though its waters were not troubled, and a pleasant odour therefrom was wafted.

Isho'dad gives this curious passage in almost the same words: it may be conjectured to have been taken from some early Hymn, perhaps one of S. Ephraim's own. Dr Harris remarks (p. 44): "It is not necessary to suppose that the whole of the extract....is from Tatian. Probably the quotation is contained in the first clause, or, at most, in the words

[Syriac text] [[Syriac]] [Syriac text]."

I have added [Syriac] from Barsalibi, though it is omitted by Isho'dad and Dr Harris, as [Syriac] [Syriac] corresponds to the Old Latin readings in Matt iii 16, where we find 'lumen ingens' in *a* and 'lumen magnum' in *g*. It may be remarked that *g* (Cod. Sangermanensis), where it differs from the majority of Latin MSS, in several instances presents us with readings attested for the Diatessaron.

The Hymns de Virginitate.

Of the numerous Hymns printed by *Lamy* at the end of his second volume very few contain allusions of textual interest. Those which are taken from such ancient MSS as B.M. Add. 14571 have been already given in this book. But many of the Hymns are only preserved in B.M. Add. 14506, a miscellaneous collection of leaves dating from the 9th to the 11th century: the passage quoted below is taken from the 11th century portion of the MS.

Lamy ii 815 = Matt iv 5, Lk iv 9

ܟܕ ܕܝܢ ܚܙ ܗܘܐ ܘܚܙܐ ܡܪܢ . ܥܠ ܪܝܫ ܩܪܢܐ ܟܕ
ܒܪܡ ܗܘܝܬ.

Now who had looked and saw thee, our Lord, on the head of the corner when thou wert standing?

The 'pinnacle' of the Temple is rendered by ܩܪܢܐ 'corner' (*lit.* 'horn') in *C* (Matt) and *S* (Lk). But the Peshitta has ܟܢܦܐ 'wing' in both Gospels, followed by *S* in S. Matthew.

The Sermones Rogationum.

These Hymns (ܕܒܥܘܬܐ) are mostly of the nature of Prayers for Rain. They are preserved in a late transcript made for Archbishop Ussher, now at Trinity College, Dublin (cod. B 5. 18), and have been edited by Lamy from this MS and from Bedjan's Chaldee Breviary. Some Hymns of this series are found in B.M. Add. 17164, *foll.* 1—15, of the 6th or 7th century, but the only Gospel allusions of textual interest occur in Hymns not covered by the extant fragments of this MS.

Lamy iii 53 = Matt vi 11, Lk xi 3

ܐܝܟ ܕܐܡܝܢ ܠܚܡܗ ܕܚܘܝܐ. ܠܚܡܐ ܐܡܝܢܐ ܗܒ ܠܢ ܡܪܝ.

As the Serpent's bread is constant, constant bread give us, my Lord!

This is an evident allusion to the 'daily bread' of the Lord's Prayer. 'Constant bread' (ܠܚܡܐ ܐܡܝܢܐ) is the rendering of ἄρτος ἐπιούσιος found in all Old Syriac authorities wherever they are extant, including the Acts of Thomas (Wright's text, p. 313); it even survives in the Homily upon the Lord's Prayer by Jacob of Serug [B.M. Add. 17157, *fol.* 38]. But the Peshitta has both in S. Matthew and S. Luke 'the bread of our need' (ܠܚܡܐ ܕܣܘܢܩܢܢ).

Lamy iii 63 = Lk xviii 13

ܗܘ ܚܛܝܐ ܠܐ ܐܡܪܚ. ܕܢܚܘܪ ܗܘܐ ܠܡ ܒܫܡܝܐ.

That sinner (it says) did not dare to be looking to heaven.

This appears to be taken from the Diatessaron: see above, p. 46.

The "Letter to Publius."

B.M. Add. 7190, a 12th century collection of miscellanies, contains on *foll.* 188—193 some extracts from the Letter of S. Ephraim to a person named Publius or Popilius.[1] Nothing is known of this individual, and the Letter does not seem to be quoted elsewhere, but the extracts are remarkable for being in prose, whereas most of what was ascribed to S. Ephraim in later times is in the familiar 7-syllable metre. The piece therefore comes before us with a certain shew of genuineness, and it is surprising that no one has ever thought it worth while to edit it. As far as I made out from a very hasty perusal, the extracts mainly consist of a kind of Vision of Judgement.

[1] *Title* ܕܩܕܝܫܐ ܡܪܝ ܐܦܪܝܡ: ܡܢ ܐܓܪܬܐ ܕܠܘܬ ܦܘܦܠܝܘܣ.

There are two quotations of textual interest from the Gospel.
(1) B.M. Add. 7190, *fol.* 189 r = Lk xvi 25

[Syriac text]

'*My son, remember that thou receivedst good things in thy life and thy folly, and Lazar received his evil things and his afflictions beforehand; and now he cannot come and help thee in thy torments, because thou didst not help him in torments and his infirmities. Therefore thou dost beseech of him to help thee, as he had besought of thee to help him, and thou wouldst not.*'

This is a free paraphrase, but one point is perfectly clear: in the last clause παρακαλεῖται is not rendered as in our Bibles "he is comforted" (or "resteth"), but "he is *besought*." The former rendering is that of the Peshitta and of *S*, while the latter is found in Aphraates and we may well believe it to be the rendering characteristic of the Diatessaron.[2] The actual words of Aphraates (*Wright*, p. 383) are

[Syriac text] (*v. l.* [Syriac]) [Syriac text].

'*My son, recollect that thou receivedst thy good things in thy life, and Lazar received his evil things: but to-day thou dost beseech of him, and he doth not help thee.*'

The only other passage I know where this view of παρακαλεῖται is taken is Cyprian *Test* III 61, in which according to the better MSS we

---

[1] Cod. [Syriac]

[2] The leaf of *C* which contained this passage is missing. It is also probable that Aphraates and Ephraim read ὅδε παρακαλεῖται with the Latins and the 'Textus Receptus,' while *S* and the Peshitta (with the great majority of Greek MSS) support ὧδε παρακαλεῖται.

read: *Commemorare quoniam percepisti bona in uita tua, Eleazar autem mala: nunc hic* ROGATUR, *tu autem doles.* The rest of the Latin texts have *consolatur.*

It is also worth remark that the word used in the letter to Publius for the χάσμα of Lk xvi 26 is ܚܘܬܐ as in Aphraates 383, but in Pesh. and *S* we find the synonym ܗܘܬܐ. Curiously enough, the Harclean has ܚܘܬܐ and a similar word is used in the Palestinian Lectionary.

(2) B.M. Add. 7190, *fol.* 190 v = Lk xii 16—20

ܠܐ ܚܙܐ ܐܢܬ ܡܢܐ ܓܕܫ ܠܝܐ ܗܘ ܕܐܥܠܬ
ܐܪܥܗ ܥܠܠܬܐ ܣܓܝܐܬܐ. ܕܐܡܪ ܠܢܦܫܗ: ܢܦܫܝ
ܐܟܘܠܝ ܘܐܫܬܝ ܘܐܬܒܣܡܝ, ܡܛܠ ܕܗܐ ܥܠܠܬܐ
ܣܓܝܐܬܐ ܣܝܡܢ ܠܟܝ ܠܫܢܝܐ ܣܓܝܐܬܐ. ܗܐ
ܒܗܢܐ ܠܠܝܐ ܢܦܫܟܝ ܚܒܝܒܬܐ ܡܢܟ ܬܒܥܝܢ ܠܗ.
ܡܕܡ ܕܛܝܒܬ ܠܟ ܕܡܢ ܗܘܐ.

Dost thou not see what befel to him whose land brought in to him much produce? Because he said to his soul: 'My soul, eat and drink and rest and be merry, because lo, much produce is stored up for thee for many years' 'Lo, in this night thy dear soul—from thee they require it: that which thou hast made ready, whose will it be?'

This Parable is quoted in Aphraates 381 in very close agreement with the extract from the Letter to Publius. In common with Aphraates and *C* against *S* and Pesh. it has 'he said to his soul' instead of 'I will say to my soul.' In common with Aphraates and Pesh. against *S* and *C* it prefixes the vocative 'Soul' to the rich man's meditation, and it has ܐܟܘܠܝ 'eat' instead of the synonym ܠܥܣܝ. But it also has in common with Aphraates against *S C* and Pesh. ܣܝܡܢ 'stored up' instead of ܣܝܡܝܢ 'laid up,' and it has ܗܘܐ. ܗܢܐ ܡܢ in the last clause instead of ܗܘܘܢ ܠܗܝܢ, i.e. singular instead of plural. It is difficult to see what cause can be assigned for this marked agreement between the 'Letter to Publius' and Aphraates against other Syriac texts, except a common use of the Diatessaron.

The Letters to Hypatius.

S. Ephraim's Letters to Hypatius upon various heresies must have been when complete one of the longest and most important of his prose works. The first book is preserved in B.M. Add. 14570, and fragments of the first and second books in B.M. Add. 14574. These MSS are of the 5th or 6th century, and from them the text has been edited in *Overbeck* 21—73. The Gospel quotations have been examined in the body of this work, pp. 29 and 46; they include a very characteristic agreement with *C* against almost all other authorities in an allusion to Lk xviii 13.

Cod. 14574 is only a fragment of nineteen leaves, but a large portion of the rest of this valuable MS still exists as a palimpsest in B.M. Add. 14623. Dr Overbeck made no attempt to edit this portion of the text, which is quite illegible in many places. I have been, however, fortunate enough to make out one important passage which throws new light upon the size and arrangement of the work.

The title of the Discourses in cod. 14574, *fol.* 1v is

Epistles of S. Ephraim to Hypatius arranged according to the letters (of the alphabet) *against False Doctrines.*

On this Wright observes (*CBM* 408): "The words ܠܘ ܦܬܓ̈ܡܐ ܐܬܘ̈ܬܐ would appear to imply that there were 22 of these discourses, each commencing with a letter of the alphabet, in the usual order, like those of Aphraates; but this seems unlikely, as the second discourse begins with the letter ܒ (ܒܘܪܟܬܐ).[1] Besides, there is no mention of alphabetical arrangement in Add. 14570."

Dr Wright's suspicions were well grounded; the true arrangement of the work may be gathered from the beginning of the Fourth Discourse, which is to be found in cod. 14623, *fol.* 27r, centre column.

---

[1] See *Overbeck* 59.

74   S. EPHRAIM'S QUOTATIONS.

We there read

        ܥܠ ܟܡܐܝܢ

        . ܗܕܬܐ .

        ooooooooooooo

        ܟܡܐܝܢ ܐܝܒܪܐ

        ܕܠܡܒܐ ܥܠܡܐ

        . ܫܠܝ .

        ܝܕܥܝܢ ܐܢܬܘܢ

Here endeth the Third Discourse.
The Fourth Discourse against False Doctrines.

Y *Ye know......*

Thus we reconstruct the contents as follows:

   The First Discourse begins   ܐ ܐܦܪܝܡ ܠܚܘܦܒܘ...

   The Second begins   ܒ ܒܐܘܪܚܐ ܕܫܘܝܢ ܥܡ...

   The beginning of the Third is lost

   The Fourth begins   ܡ ܝܕܥܝܢ ܐܢܬܘܢ...

When the facts are thus tabulated, it does not require a great stretch of imagination to conjecture that the Letters to Hypatius were not 22 in number but 5, and that they were arranged in the order of the five letters of the author's name ܐܦܪܝܡ.

A similar method of signature is actually used by S. Ephraim in the Hymn added at the end of the Hymns on Paradise (*Overbeck* 351 ff.), the several stanzas of which begin with the letters ܐ ܒ ܝ ܡ.

It is a pity that the palimpsest fragments of S. Ephraim in B.M. Add. 14623 are still unedited. The writing is perfectly legible in some places, though no doubt there are passages which were only too successfully deleted early in the 9th century by the individual whom Wright calls "the miserable monk Aaron" (*CBM* 766). As far as I can make out, the Letters to Hypatius are mainly directed against the teaching of Bardaisan and his School, while the Letters to Domnus, fragments of which also survive in B.M. Add. 14623, are directed against Marcion.

APPENDIX III.

On some writings commonly ascribed to S. Ephraim which have been rejected in this Essay.

In the previous Appendix some writings have been discussed which seem to be genuine works of S. Ephraim, but do not happen to be sufficiently well attested in extant MSS to be included in the body of this Essay. In the present section I propose to examine a few of the more noteworthy of those writings in which the sum of the evidence, internal or external, is not merely insufficient to establish Ephraimitic authorship but actually adverse to it.

The Tractates in B.M. Add. 17189.

These Tractates are all printed by Overbeck (pp. 74—104), and consist of prose expositions of various passages of Scripture. Together with these expositions, or *Turgâmé*, is a Homily on Fasting, which has been printed by Lamy (vol. iii 707—717) as well as by Overbeck. B.M. Add. 17189, the manuscript in which these writings are preserved, is of the 5th or 6th century and (so far as I can find out) no trace of them is known to survive elsewhere. I have been led to exclude them from the list of genuine works of S. Ephraim partly by the weakness of the external evidence and partly by the unfavourable testimony of the writings themselves.

In the first place it is improbable that the original scribe of cod. 17189 ascribed them to S. Ephraim. Dr William Wright says in his description of the MS (*CBM* 407):—"The title, fol. 1*b*, has been effaced, and in its place we now read the following mutilated words, written by a later hand: ܐܬܐ (*sic*) ܒܝܢ... ܩܝܣܐܬ ܐܝܢܐ... ܩܘܪܒܢܐ ܐܘ ܡܠܠܘܬܐ; which seem to imply that the writer ascribed these homilies, not to Ephraim, but to Basil or John

Chrysostom. However, on fol. 9*a* we can still read the partially effaced running title ܕܡܪܝ ܐܦܪܝܡ; and again, on foll. 12*b* and 13*a*, ܕܡܪܝ ܐܦܪܝܡ ܗܘܿܬܠܐ; besides (sic) ܕܡܪܝ ܐܦܪ on the margin of fol. 2*a* in a later hand."

But a close inspection of the MS has convinced me that the headings which assign the pieces to S. Ephraim were not inserted by the original scribe. The headlines on *foll.* 12 v, 13 r run

   (*fol.* 13 r)   (*fol.* 12 v)

  ·o· ܐܦܪܝܡ, ܕܡܪܝ ·o· ··o· ܗܘܿܬܠܐ ·o··

The letters on *fol.* 12 v are undoubtedly contemporary with the rest of the book. But those on *fol.* 13 r are larger and stiffer than the ܗܘܿܬܠܐ on the opposite page, and the ornament at the beginning and end of the inscription is different to that on *fol.* 12 v. Whether the original hand wrote any headlines on the left-hand side cannot now be ascertained; possibly the only heading was ܗܘܿܬܠܐ, i.e. 'Expositions,' on the right-hand side.

On *fol.* 1 v there are two inscriptions prefixed to the first 'exposition' as a title to the whole volume. The older one, by the same hand that wrote 'Of S. Ephraim' for the headline to *fol.* 13 r, has been almost entirely washed out and it is not given by Wright. But it is still possible to decipher the words

  ܟܬܒܐ ܐܦܪܝܡ, ܕܡܪܝ ܕܬܘܪܓܡܐ ܛܘܒܢܐ

   A Tome of Discourses of the blessed S. Ephraim.

This inscription was washed out by the later hand that wrote the note given by Wright and quoted above. This note is unfortunately not preserved in full owing to the mutilation of the top of the page. It is a rather ugly Estrangela scrawl, not like the writing of a professional scribe.

Thus we learn from a study of the MS that no evidence survives to shew to whom the writings in B.M. Add. 17189 were assigned by the original scribe; we learn also that they were ascribed to S. Ephraim by a much later hand, but that a still later scholar considered them to be the work of S. Basil or S. Chrysostom.

When we turn to the Expositions themselves there is really not very much evidence from their style as to date or authorship. The writer is convinced that the Tree of the Knowledge of Good and Evil was a Fig-tree, "than which there is none better for food" (*Overbeck* 82²¹ᶠ). The Biblical quotations, however, are inconsistent with a Syriac origin. Most of them indeed are assimilated to the Peshitta, especially in the Psalms,[1] while on the other hand the references to S. Paul, which were less familiar, present variations from all known Syriac texts.[2] But the really decisive case occurs in a discourse on the Fall, the writer quoting Gen iii 15 with an exposition which makes it clear that he used not the Peshitta but the Greek Bible. He says (*Overbeck* 87¹⁷⁻²⁵) :—

"Wherefore God also thus said unto the serpent, while with the same words that He was saying He was making known the sentence upon the Devil : '*He shall observe thy head and thou shalt observe his heel.*'[3] The significance of His word being : 'This man whom thou hast led astray, if so be that he direct his gaze toward good things, it damageth thee much that he hath dominion over thee and is made strong ; but thou shalt be able to hurt him, if so be that when thou art observing the courses of his life thou shalt find that he chooseth evil…' "

It cannot be doubted that the writer of this read Gen iii 15 according to the LXX rendering αὐτός σου τηρήσει κεφαλὴν καὶ σὺ τηρήσεις αὐτοῦ πτέρναν, and not as in the Peshitta, which has both in the printed editions and in S. Ephraim's Commentary (*Ed. Rom.* iv 36 A) *He shall trample on thy head and thou shalt strike at his heel.*[4]

It follows, as a necessary corollary, that these Expositions are not the work of S. Ephraim, or indeed of any native Syriac writer, but are translations from the Greek. The doubts of the author of the Note given by Wright are thus amply justified.

The quotations from the Gospel in the writings contained in B.M. Add. 17189 are :—

---

[1] See especially *Ov.* 103²⁰ᶠᶠ, where Pss lxxviii 34, xxxiv 1, 2, cvi 3, are quoted in succession. The reference to Ps lxxviii (lxxvii) 34 was missed by Lamy (vol. ii 715), with unfortunate results.

[2] E.g. the reference to Gal vi 9 in *Overbeck* 102².

[3] The Syriac here is ܡܢܐ ܐܝܟ ܕܘܟܐ . ܝܬܝܪ ܐܝܟ ܪܢ ܗܘ.

[4] In Syriac ܡܢܐ ܢܣܘܚܕ ܕܘܟܐ . ܝܬܝܪ ܟܣܢ ܗܘ

S. EPHRAIM'S QUOTATIONS.

1. Matt vi 33 = *Overbeck* 104

[Syriac text]

'*For seek first the kingdom of God and His righteousness, and these all besides are added to you.*'

Here [Syriac] is the order found in *C*; but the participle [Syriac] is the reading of Pesh., *C* having the future.

2. Matt vii 7 = *Overbeck* 102

[Syriac text]

'*For every one that asketh receiveth, and he which seeketh findeth, and he which knocketh—it is opened to him.*'

Here [Syriac] agrees with Pesh., while *C* has [Syriac] in both places, the sense being unaltered.

3. Matt x 25 = *Overbeck* 98

[Syriac text]

If the Master of the house they have called Beelzebub, how much rather the sons of his house will they call drunkards?

The last word is of course a reference to Acts ii 13 ff., the passage which is being explained. The reference to Matt x 25 is, however, interesting for our purpose, as the occurrence of the specifically Syriac spelling Beelzebub (for Beelzebul) shews that the Biblical quotations have been more or less influenced by the current Syriac version.

4. Lk x 19 = *Overbeck* 95

[Syriac text]

Be trampling on serpents and scorpions and all the power of the enemy.

This agrees with the Peshitta, while S and C have ܢܗܘܘܢ 'ye shall be,' instead of ܗܘܝܬܘܢ.

Besides these four quotations there are allusions of no textual interest in *Overbeck* 95 to Mk xvi 17 and Joh xvi 33.

The Homilies 'De Magis' and 'De Fine et Admonitione.'

The determination of the authorship and date of these two Homilies is perhaps a more delicate problem than meets us in any other of the works which have been issued under the name of S. Ephraim. It is convenient to take them together, as the style and contents of the two discourses suggest that they are in any case the work of the same author, the *De Fine et Admonitione* following the *De Magis*.

1. *External Evidence.*—The Homily 'De Magis, Incantoribus et Divinis, et de Fine et Consummatione' is edited in *Lamy* ii 393—425. It is written in 7-syllable metre, the first line being ܡܢ ܕܝܢ ܪܚܡ ܠܐܠܗܐ. It is found in four MSS, viz:

B.M. Add. 14615 (*saec.* x°, xi°)   [*Wright*, p. 840]
B.M. Add. 14650 (AD 875)   [*Wright*, p. 1105]
B.M. Add. 7190 (*saec.* xii°)   [*Wright*, p. 1206]
Oxon. *Marsh* 711 (*saec.* xvii°)

Two errors made by Dr Lamy in describing these MSS may be conveniently pointed out here. In ii 312, par. 4, cod. 14650 is stated to be of the 6th or 7th century. This is only true of foll. 1—8 and 30—68. The rest of the MS, including the leaves on which the Homily *De Magis* is written, was written at Dulichium, N.E. of Antioch, in the year 875 AD (Wright, *CBM* 1103). Again, Dr Lamy's statement in ii 393 that the Homily is found in a Vatican MS and ascribed to Isaac of Antioch refers not to our Homily, but to the Homily on Isaiah xl 6, printed by Lamy on col. 313 ff.[1]

The Homily 'De Fine et Admonitione' is edited in *Lamy* iii 133—185. It also is written in 7-syllable metre, the first line being ܐܠܐ ܐܚܝ ܗܘ ܠܝ ܐܚܐ. It is found in three MSS, viz:

B.M. Add. 14590 (*saec.* viii°, ix°)   [*Wright*, p. 752]
Oxon. *Marsh* 711 (*saec.* xvii°)
B.N. Paris. 13

Of these, Paris. 13 is merely a fragment.

---

[1] This Homily on Isaiah is certainly by S. Isaac: see Wright, *CBM* 675, 734.

Thus there is no extant evidence for either Homily earlier than the end of the 8th century. The MSS in which they are found are with one exception of miscellaneous contents, not regular collections of S. Ephraim's writings. One of them, cod. 7190, was partly copied from the Nitrian MS of the so-called "Zacharias Rhetor," as is pointed out by Wright, *CBM* 1047, 1206; so that there is considerable probability that its text of the *De Magis* was copied from cod. 14650, together with "the history of Paul the priest and his disputation with Satan" and some other biographical notices.

The critical value of the 17th century Oxford MS, the only one in which both Homilies are given, is somewhat lessened by the fact that it includes a tract "of S. Ephraim" against the *Nestorians*. On this Dr Overbeck quaintly observed (p. xxii): "Nescio an codex noster minoris sit fidei, quum fol. 65 Ephraemi Liber adversus Nestorianos, Ephraemo plus quinquaginta annis posteriores, proponatur."[1]

It may also be remarked that cod. 14590, the only MS of respectable age that contains the *De Fine et Admonitione*, seems to have been copied from a MS in which this Homily was not counted among the rest of S. Ephraim's Homilies. In its present state the only Ephraimitic work preserved in cod. 14590 is the end of the *De Fine et Admonitione* itself. But a rubric of contents, quoted by Wright, *CBM* 753, says:

"In this tome are (the following) Homilies: 1st, On the End; on Matt xxiv 20; On Ananias and Sapphira; On the Rich Man and Lazarus; On Repentance; On the Kingdom of Gehenna, by Mar Ephraim;

On the End and Admonition, and shewing how the righteous and the sinners are rewarded on the Day of Resurrection, and how the righteous inherit the Kingdom of Heaven and the wicked (inherit) the Fire and the weeping and gnashing of teeth, by Mar Ephraim; [*This is our De Fine*]

On Job; on the Blasphemer; on the Labourers; on the City of Antioch; etc."

The last set of Homilies are by Jacob of Serug. I have abbreviated the titles of the other Homilies, but they are none of them so long as that to the *De Fine*, which though ascribed to S. Ephraim is clearly added on at the end of the list of his Homilies in a separate category.

---

[1] The meagre selection of variants given by Lamy gives no idea of the extent to which *Marsh* 711 differs from the printed text. Thus for instance it entirely omits § 7 of the *De Magis* (*Lamy* ii 415), inserting in its place a commemoration of the Twelve Minor Prophets and of the Four Evangelists!

2. *Internal Evidence.*—A careful study of the two Homilies has left me with the impression that they were composed at Antioch after the time of S. Chrysostom, i.e. not earlier than the 5th century. The most striking point common to both Homilies is the curse pronounced upon those who 'eat with the Jews.'

"He that eateth with the magicians shall not eat the body of our Lord, and he that drinketh with the enchanters shall not drink the blood of the Messiah, and he that eateth with the Jews shall not inherit life eternal" (De Magis, *Lamy* ii 399).

"Every one that hath eaten and drunken and mingled with the Jews entereth thither into the accusation that he hath become the comrade of the crucifiers" (De Magis, *Lamy* ii 411).

"I have pondered what is the judgement of him that eateth the sacrifice of a pagan, and into what accusation he entereth who eateth with the Jews" (De Fine, *Lamy* iii 137).

"Great woe in that day to him that hath eaten with the Jews, and hath adorned himself with the garb of the Gentiles, for with them he doth inherit torment!" (De Fine, *Lamy* iii 165).

The Homilist does not seem to think it worth while to explain more fully the nature of this curious offence: evidently therefore 'to eat with the Jews' must have been a well understood phrase. It does not occur in any of the undoubtedly genuine works of S. Ephraim, nor does he anywhere exhibit special animosity against the Jews. But the sin of frequenting Jewish synagogues and of keeping fast and festival with the Jews is the main theme of S. Chrysostom's eight discourses *Adversus Judaeos*, delivered at Antioch AD 386. "Many," he says in the first discourse, "of those enrolled in our ranks and professing to share our beliefs betake themselves to the Synagogues; some, no doubt, merely go to look on at the festival, but others actually feast with the Jews and join in their fasts. This evil custom I intend now to banish from the Church" (*Migne* xlviii 844).[1] "I fear," he says again, "lest some out of ignorance partake of their transgression" (*Ibid.* 845). "Dost thou fast with the Jews? Take thy shoes off also with them, and imitate their unseemly gestures" (*Ibid.* 849). There can be little

---

[1] The last clause runs in the original καὶ τοῦτο τὸ πονηρὸν ἔθος βούλομαι τῆς Ἐκκλησίας ἀπέλασαι νῦν. The whole tone of the passage gives the impression of a reformer attacking an abuse for the first time.

doubt that 'to eat with the Jews' means to the author of the *De Magis* and the *De Fine* the offence of these Antiochene Christians, who kept the Jewish ecclesiastical year.

It may be added that in these same discourses *Adversus Judaeos* S. Chrysostom refers to the Parables of the Ten Virgins and of the Man that had not on a Wedding Garment as in the *De Fine* (*Ibid.* 868), and goes on to attack the custom of wearing charms and amulets— ἐπῳδαί and περίαπτα—as in the *De Magis* (*Ibid.* 938). Some at least of these discourses of S. Chrysostom were translated into Syriac (Wright, *CBM* 763, 764), but even apart from formal translations the sermons of the golden-mouthed orator may very well have provided the Christian congregations of Antioch with Anti-semite watchwords.

A further parallel to S. Chrysostom is afforded by the twice-repeated woe pronounced in the *De Fine* against those who go out of church on Sunday before the end of the Communion Service. "Great woe in that day to him that on the first day of the week leaveth Christ sacrificed and sitteth in the market-place!" (*Lamy* iii 155). And again: "Great woe in that day to him that sitteth in the market-place at the moment when the priest calleth the Holy Spirit to come down upon him!" (*Ibid.* 159). A homily of S. Chrysostom's upon this very topic survives in a Syriac translation (Wright, *CBM* 695, 888). The same subject is treated of by Jacob of Serug and by Isaac of Antioch, but it finds, so far as I know, no echo in S. Ephraim.

The attack made by the author of the *De Magis* on the practice of wearing amulets containing magical writings as a protection against disease affords a parallel with the homilies of Isaac of Antioch even closer and more remarkable than any of those with S. Chrysostom. These amulets seem to have been much used by the Antiochenes and S. Chrysostom had gone so far as to say that the man who fell a victim to disease through refusing to carry such things about him ought to be counted as a Christian martyr.[1] A particularly offensive feature of the amulets was that the names of demons were often inscribed upon them in juxtaposition with the names of angels, with words of Scripture or the most sacred titles of God. "The wizards and enchanters lead

---

[1] Εὖγε εὖγε ὦ ἄνθρωπε, ὁ Χριστοῦ δοῦλος, ὁ πιστὸς ἀνήρ, ὁ ἀθλητὴς τῆς εὐσεβείας, ὁ τοῖς δεινοῖς αἱρούμενος ἐναποθανεῖν μᾶλλον ἢ προδοῦναι τὴν ἐγχειρισθεῖσαν εὐσέβειαν, μετὰ τῶν μαρτύρων στήσῃ κατ' ἐκείνην τὴν ἡμέραν (*Migne* xlviii 938).

REJECTED WRITINGS. 83

astray this foolish people, mixing blasphemy with the very words of the Holy Spirit. After impiously writing the Name of Father, Son, and Spirit, they attach thereto the names of demons and defile the holiness of the Names" (*Isaac* xxxiv 531—534).[1] "They enter and say in the midst of the Church *Deliver us, O Lord, from the Evil One* : why, the Evil One is hanging round their neck, and yet they pray for deliverance!" (*De Magis*, p. 395).

The above quotations, though similar in tone, do not imply literary connexion : it is otherwise with the next pair, which I give in parallel columns to shew the resemblance.

'De Magis' (*Lamy* ii 395 f.)	Isaac of Antioch (*Bickell* xxxiv 479—490)
The *names* of *two angels* are in the Old Testament and the New, *Gabriel* and *Michael*, ministers *of fire and spirit*, and *the great vision of Daniel* by these two was explained. But filthy and abominable priests fly for refuge to the names of *demons*, Rufael and Rafufael, ministers of Satan[2]...	*Two angels* did *the great vision of Daniel name* for us, *Michael* and *Gabriel*, names *of fire and* of *spirit* : but at the present time, when prophets vexed by *demons* abound, a myriad names are bandied about between old wives and spinning girls. Wizards and enchanters have written the name of devils like angels, and like precious necklaces they are carried on the neck of women.

It would be a delicate task to determine which of these passages is the original and which the copy ; indeed, I have a strong suspicion that they are the work of the same author. But this at least is clear: the author of the *De Magis* went beyond the regular Syriac canon of the New Testament. Michael is mentioned in Jude 9 and Apoc xii 7, but neither of these books is included in the Peshitta. The only reference to the Apocalypse in S. Ephraim's works occurs in a Homily

[1] Bickell's Edition, vol. ii, p. 188.
[2] *Rufael* (ܪܘܦܐܝܠ) and *Rafufael* (ܪܦܘܦܐܝܠ) are probably to be identified with the angels Raphael and Rahabiel, whose work, according to a Jewish magical work published by Dr M. Gaster in the *Proceedings* of the Society of Biblical Archaeology for Dec. 1900, is "to cure all manner of disease, to preserve man from all wicked Shiddim and from all evil spirits which cause illness to man."

ascribed to him upon ludicrously insufficient evidence.[1] On the other hand a Syriac writer living like S. Isaac at Antioch, in the midst of a Greek community, would more easily become acquainted with Christian books outside those recognised as canonical among his countrymen.

I venture to think that these parallels of thought and wording with S. Chrysostom and Isaac of Antioch are sufficient to raise a very serious presumption against the Ephraimitic authorship of the *De Magis* and the *De Fine*. It must however be noted that the *De Magis*, at least according to the transmitted text, professes to be the work of "Ephraim." The latter part of this homily describes the last judgement, and ends thus:

"One will be in the midst of Paradise, and one they will cast outside; one is glorified and perfected and holy, and with him doth God dwell: for every man according to his work receiveth wage from Justice. They beseech thee, O God, the Hope of all the saints—*make thy mercy shine upon Ephraim, in that day when mercy is needed, for I am not worthy to enter the kingdom, I that am a sinner. Round about the tabernacle of thy saints make me worthy to be and it sufficeth for me, and I will send up praise and thanksgiving for ever and ever. Amen, amen.*"

The portion printed in italics does not fit on to the rest, and may very well have been added—possibly from another poem of Ephraim's—by an editor who ascribed it to him and found the work imperfect at the end.[2] It may also be remarked that S. Ephraim's custom was to indicate his authorship by an acrostic, not by giving his name in full at the end. This is done, for example, in the case of the Hymn added at the end of the *Paradise* (printed by Overbeck, pp. 351—354), and in the five books addressed to Hypatius.

There are no quotations from any part of the New Testament in the *De Magis*, except the implied reference to the Epistle of Jude or the Apocalypse which has just been mentioned.

---

[1] See above, p. 22.

[2] As a matter of fact, cod. 14615, one of the two leading MSS of the *De Magis*, is actually mutilated here.

The *De Fine* contains express allusions to the Parable of the Man who had not on a Wedding-Garment (Matt xxii 11 ff.), and to the Parable of the Wise and Foolish Virgins (Matt xxv 1 ff.). With regard to the latter it is noticeable that there is no mention of the Bride, although according both to the Peshitta and the *Evangelion da-Mepharreshe* the virgins "went forth to meet the bridegroom *and the bride.*" The allusion in *Lamy* iii 143 is, however, too paraphrastic to be at all decisive.

But there can be no doubt as to the text of Matt xxii 13 attested by the *De Fine.* We read (*Lamy* iii 139):

ܘܐܣܪܝܢ ܠܗ ܒܐܝܕܘܗܝ، ܘܒܪ̈ܓܠܘܗܝ، ܘܡܦܩܝܢ ܠܗ ܒܐܬܪܐ ܕܚܫܘܟܐ.

And they bind him by his hands and his feet, and cast him out in the place of darkness.

And again (*Lamy* iii 147):

ܘܐܝ̈ܕܝܟ ܘܪ̈ܓܠܝܟ ܐܣܪܝܢ ܠܟ. ܘܡܦܩܝܢ ܠܟ ܠܐܬܪܐ ܕܚܫܘܟܐ.

And thy hands and thy feet they bind for thee, and cast thee out into the place of darkness.

In this verse there is a well-marked various reading. The Peshitta, following ℵB and the text generally approved by modern critical editors has ܐܣܘܪܘ ܐܝ̈ܕܘܗܝ ܘܪ̈ܓܠܘܗܝ 'Bind his hands and his feet.' Both *S* and *C*, on the other hand, have ܐܚܘܕܘܗܝ ܒܐܝ̈ܕܘܗܝ ܘܒܪ̈ܓܠܘܗܝ 'Take hold of him by his hands and his feet,' a rendering which probably represents the 'Western' reading ἄρατε αὐτὸν ποδῶν καὶ χειρῶν. The distribution of evidence is, however, complicated by the fact that in an allusion to Matt xxii 13 in the Acts of Thomas (*Wright*, p. 315) we find ܠܐ ܢܦܟܪܘܢ ܐܝ̈ܕܝ ܘܪ̈ܓܠܝ 'Let them not fetter my hands and my feet.' The other Gospel quotations and allusions in the Syriac Acts of Thomas appear to be taken from the *Evangelion da-Mepharreshe.* They seem to be independent of the Diatessaron and are certainly uninfluenced by the Peshitta. The use of ܦܟܪ is also supported by the allusion to this passage in Ephraim's *Carmina Nisibena,* which has been discussed above, p. 35. It is possible therefore that the reading which speaks of the man being *fettered*, and not merely *seized* or *carried*, was current in early Syriac Biblical MSS.[1]

The allusions in the *De Fine* give the verb ܐܚܕ, the same that is used in the Peshitta, and it is doubtless the Peshitta text that was in the mind of the author. But I hope to have convinced my readers that no conclusions with regard to the Biblical text used by S. Ephraim could be drawn either from that Homily or from its companion the *De Magis*.

The Severus Catena.

The fact that no quotations from the New Testament occur in the *Story of Joseph* saves me from the necessity of investigating the authorship of that dull and long-winded composition, The only parts of it which are extant in ancient MSS are there ascribed to Balai the Chorepiscopus or to Jacob of Serug. Later Syriac tradition, represented by the *Book of the Bee* and some recent MSS, make S. Ephraim the author. This view is accepted by Dr Lamy, who has edited the whole ten books in his third volume. As a rule, when a work is ascribed to a famous writer (such as S. Ephraim) in late documents and to a less famous writer (such as Mar Balai) in an early document, it is generally safe to assume that the late documents have got their information by way of unverified conjecture.

There is also no necessity for examining one by one the numerous writings ascribed to S. Ephraim in MSS of the 12th century or later. A few of them may be genuine, others may contain a genuine nucleus adapted for liturgical use (as in many of the *Necrosima*). But in such matters internal evidence alone can be our guide. A minute and careful search might perhaps add a little to our knowledge of Ephraim's New Testament, but the character of its text could not be changed by 12th century evidence; on the contrary, I am not afraid to make the character of the Gospel quotations a touchstone of genuineness.

---

[1] Compare also the quotation in Eus. *Theoph*^{yr} iv 16, which runs

ܐܚܝܕ ܐܢܫܐ ܘܐܚܝܕ܀

Where the Gospel quotations in these badly attested writings agree with the *Diatessaron* or the *Evangelion da-Mepharreshe* we may believe S. Ephraim to be the writer, but agreement in them with the Peshitta is a sign not that S. Ephraim used the Peshitta, but that the writing is not S. Ephraim's.

The *Severus Catena* might be dismissed on these grounds without further remark. As however it is the source from which the greater number of those quotations come which have been brought forward to prove the use of the Peshitta by S. Ephraim I think I ought not to conclude this Essay without saying a few words about it.

The Commentary upon Genesis and Exodus printed in the Roman Edition, vol. iv, pp. 1—115, 194—225, is undoubtedly a genuine work of S. Ephraim. It is extant in a MS of the 6th century (Vat. Syr. cx), and the three Gospel quotations found in it are marked by the usual characteristics of S. Ephraim's allusions.[1] But the Commentaries upon the rest of the Old Testament published under the name of S. Ephraim are not taken direct from his works. They are excerpts from a *Catena Patrum* compiled by one Severus, a monk of Edessa, in 861 AD.[2] Of this Catena there are two MSS, Vat. Syr. ciii and B.M. Add. 12144 (written AD 1081): what we read in the Roman Edition iv 116—193, 226—571, v 1—315, is taken from the Vatican MS, and this is supplemented from the British Museum MS in *Lamy* ii 105—310.

It is evident at the first glance that in the Catena of Severus we are dealing with a state of the text quite different from that in the genuine Commentaries of S. Ephraim. The Catena is made up of extracts and abstracts from many writers, including Jacob of Edessa and Greek Fathers such as S. Basil. It is often impossible to discover where the passages taken from S. Ephraim really begin or end, and even if a given passage be accepted as S. Ephraim's there is generally nothing to shew that a Biblical quotation occurring in it may not have been supplied or edited by Severus. In *Lamy* ii 239 S. Ephraim is made to discuss renderings of Aquila and Symmachus, which I am sure any one familiar with his genuine style will consider exceedingly improbable.

---

[1] See above, pp. 32, 48, 54.
[2] Wright's *Syriac Literature* 35, and *CBM* 912.

88   S. EPHRAIM'S QUOTATIONS.

The mixed character of the text may be sufficiently illustrated by a few specimens.

(a) Definitely Peshitta readings.

Rom. v 174 c = Matt v 28

[Syriac text]

Like that (saying) 'He that shall see a woman so as to long for her, immediately hath committed adultery with her in his heart.'[1]

This entirely agrees with the Peshitta, except that Pesh. has [Syriac]. But *S* and *C* have [Syriac] for [Syriac], and they omit [Syriac].

Rom. v 315 D = Matt xi 14

[Syriac text]

If ye are willing, receive that he is Elijah who is about to come.[1]

This exactly agrees with the Peshitta, but *S* and *C* have [Syriac] instead of [Syriac], *i.e. S* and *C* support the ordinary reading δέξασθαι, while Severus and Pesh. attest the itacism δέξασθε which is found in a good many inferior Greek MSS.

Other instances of Peshitta readings in the Severus Catena are *Rom.* iv 463 F (= Matt v 44)[2]; *Rom.* iv 493 D (= Matt xxv 6)[3]; *Rom.* iv 511 B (= Lk xxiii 2)[3]; *Rom.* iv 505 E (= Lk xxiv 49)[3]; *Rom.* iv 446 B (= Joh v 22)[2]; *Rom.* iv 524 D (= Joh vii 38)[2]; *Rom.* iv 560 F (= Joh viii 44)[2]; *Lamy* ii 179 (= Matt iv 17).

(b) Agreements with *S C*.

Rom. v 90 D = Matt xii 18 ; *cf* Matt iii 17, xvii 5, Lk iii 22.

· *This is my Son and my Beloved.*'[1]

See above, p. 28.

[1] Verified from B.M. 12144.
[2] B.M. 12144 is not extant.
[3] B.M. 12144 has no quotation at this point from the Gospels.

REJECTED WRITINGS.

Rom. v 90 D = Joh iii 34

ܠܐ ܗܘܐ ܒܡܫܚܐ ܝܗܒ ܐܠܗܐ ܪܘܚܐ ܠܒܪܗ

'*Not by measure hath God given the Spirit to his Son.*'³

Here, as has been pointed out above, pp. 50, 51, Pesh. omits ܠܒܪܗ 'to his Son' with the ordinary Greek text, but the word is found in *C* and in Aphraates 123, and also in Ephraim's own comment on the passage (*Moes.* 105). This passage also illustrates the way in which the Severus Catena assimilates the text to the Peshitta, for both *S* and *C*, as well as Aphraates and Ephraim himself elsewhere (*Lamy* i 267), all use the fem. form ܡܫܚܬܐ for 'measure,' instead of ܡܫܚܐ.

Lamy ii 147 = Joh viii 48

ܠܐ ܫܦܝܪ ܐܡܪܝܢ ܚܢܢ ܕܫܡܪܝܐ ܐܢܬ ܘܕܝܘܐ ܐܝܬ ܥܠܝܟ

'*Say we not well that thou art a Samaritan, and a demon is upon thee?*'

This agrees exactly with *S*, but Pesh. has ܩܢܐ ܐܢܬ ܠܟ for δαιμόνιον ἔχεις. The variation is characteristic, for *S* has the same preposition in Joh viii 49, 52, x 20; Lk viii 27, etc.

Rom. v 166 E, *Lamy* ii (155), 186 = Matt xvi 18

ܡܘܟܠܐ ܕܫܝܘܠ

The gate-bars of Sheol.

See above, p. 30.

These last examples shew that there still remains a genuine element of S. Ephraim's quotations in the Catena. But it is impossible to gauge its extent, and certainly hazardous to draw any conclusion from the Catena as to Ephraim's use of any particular recension of the Biblical text. To borrow the words of Mr A. E. Brooke when speaking of the Commentaries of Origen (*Fragments of Heracleon*, pp. 19, 20), we may say that most of the fragments in the Catena "might have come from [*S. Ephraim's*] pen, so far as opinions are concerned. But in the comparatively few instances where they cover common ground with the extant Commentaries, the text and even the contents are either wholly different or widely divergent....The sense of lost parts of the Commentaries may be recovered, but not much of the actual text."

INDEX OF PASSAGES EXAMINED.

Those marked with an asterisk are from works not by S. Ephraim.

S. Matthew			S. Matthew (*cont.*)	
iii	16	p. 67 f.	xxvi 13	p. 36
	17	28, 88*	xxvii 46	36
iv	5	69		
v	18	67		
	28	88*	**S. Mark**	
	39	28		
vi	11	70	i 11	28
	33	78*	iv 39	37
vii	7	78*	vii 28	37
ix	17	28	33	38
x	25	78*	xii 42	39
xi	14	88*		
	19	29		
xii	18	88*		
	22	22*, note	**S. Luke**	
xiv	28 ff.	29	ii 30	40
xv	27	37	34	40
xvi	2, 3	44	36	41
	18	30, 89*	iii 22	28, 88*
	19	30	iv 9	69
xviii	12 f.	30	29	41
	22	31	vi 29	28
xxi	3	32	vii 14	42
	40, 41	34	34	29
xxii	13	35, 85*	41–43	42
xxiii	8	36	ix 62	43

INDEX.

S. Luke (cont.)			S. John	
x 19	p. 78*		i 1	p. 48, 62 ff.
xi 3	70		3	48, 59 ff.
xii 16–20	72		14	49, 63
49	44		iii 34	50, 89*
54–56	44		vi 52	51
xiv 31	45		viii 48	89*
xv 4, 5	30		xii 2	51
xvi 25	71		xiii 5	52
xvii 21	21*		xiv 23	52
31, 32	45		xv 1	53
xviii 13	46, 70		xvi 11	54
xxii 43, 44	46		xvii 11	54
xxiii 38	47		xix 30	55
43	47		xx 24	55

ولله الفتح

www.ingramcontent.com/pod-product-compliance
Lightning Source LLC
Chambersburg PA
CBHW080425210426
R18171700001B/R181717PG43193CBX00027B/41